W9-CTC-432

OpenShift for Developers
A Guide for Impatient Beginners

Grant Shipley and Graham Dumpleton

Beijing · Boston · Farnham · Sebastopol · Tokyo

OpenShift for Developers

by Grant Shipley and Graham Dumpleton

Copyright © 2016 Red Hat, Inc. All rights reserved.

Printed in the United States of America.

Published by O'Reilly Media, Inc., 1005 Gravenstein Highway North, Sebastopol, CA 95472.

O'Reilly books may be purchased for educational, business, or sales promotional use. Online editions are also available for most titles (*http://safaribooksonline.com*). For more information, contact our corporate/institutional sales department: 800-998-9938 or *corporate@oreilly.com*.

Editors: Brian MacDonald and Heather Scherer	**Interior Designer:** David Futato
Production Editor: Melanie Yarbrough	**Cover Designer:** Randy Comer
Copyeditor: Christina Edwards	**Illustrator:** Rebecca Demarest

June 2016:   First Edition

Revision History for the First Edition
2016-05-18:   First Release

978-1-491-94300-7

[LSI]

Table of Contents

Foreword

Our industry is changing. It no longer matters what type of company you work for. It no longer matters what industry you are in. Software is becoming the tool on which the futures of our companies are built, both small and large.

At the center of this change is the evolution of software development itself. Open source development models have taken over. Agile practices are needed as the pace at which one needs to respond to competition or changes in the market is relentless. Linux containers have exploded onto the market as the new basis on which to build connections between development and operations. And harnessing infrastructure for your application, from public cloud to private infrastructure, is a necessity.

For some, it can feel like the pace of change is so fast that it's better to not change at all. Having been lucky enough to participate in many of the aforementioned changes, I can assure you this is not a good position. Those who find the way to harness these changes are disrupting entire industries. It will soon be a necessity, not an option to chart your course.

When we set out to build OpenShift, this was our goal. We wanted a way for software developers to take their new idea and make it a reality. We wanted to bring them the latest technology to use to their advantage in a simple way so their energy could be focused on their idea. To be this guide for developers, we have also had to constantly evolve in support of this mission.

Grant Shipley has been at the center of our evolution. He has been our link to the developers and our guide in keeping our focus on our end users. His passion for open source and his passion for development come through in everything he does. I've watched as Grant has grown from a innovative software developer to an amazing speaker and champion of our product and mission. He's done an inspiring job of capturing that spirit in this book and I truly thank him for continuing to drive us in our mission.

Graham Dumpleton has come to us from the Python developer community where he has been a key contributor in the area of Python web application deployment. He was the author of the Apache module called mod_wsgi, a popular choice among Python developers for deploying their web applications. Graham is using all that experience to help drive forward improvements in our support for Python in OpenShift as well as our build systems based around Source-to-Image (S2I).

They both bring a wealth of experience to this book and I hope it helps propel you to that next great idea.

— Matt Hicks
VP, Engineering at Red Hat

Introduction

OpenShift has been available since 2011 and has seen great success as a polyglot platform for the deployment of web applications and services. Part of the success of OpenShift derives from the use of containers in conjunction with a Security-Enhanced Linux (SELinux) environment. These technologies enable OpenShift to implement a secure multi tenant environment suitable for the enterprise, as well as OpenShift Online, Red Hat's own public platform as a service (PaaS) offering.

Technology is always evolving, and to keep up with the latest advances OpenShift has also evolved. The latest version of OpenShift takes advantage of newer technologies such as Docker and Kubernetes, for managing and running applications within containers. Building on Kubernetes and OpenShift's own magic sauce, OpenShift takes PaaS to a new level, what we like to call a container application platform.

OpenShift offers you the ability to easily deploy your web application code directly using a library of pre-defined image builders, or you can bring your own Docker images. With support in OpenShift for features such as persistent volumes, you are not limited to just running 12-factor or cloud native applications. You can also deploy databases and many legacy applications which you otherwise would not be able to run on a traditional PaaS.

OpenShift is the modern take on PaaS that you can use with your current applications, but which also provides the power and flexibility to meet future needs. This book will bring you up to speed on how OpenShift has changed to meet the new requirements for building, deploying and hosting your applications.

Who Should Read This Book

If you are impatient, this book is for you. It is intended for programmers who want to get started using OpenShift as quickly as possible, but also want to understand a little bit of what they are doing.

We will step you through how to build and deploy your first application, and also introduce you to the main concepts of OpenShift and the tools available for working with OpenShift.

As the title indicates, we are assuming little in the way of background knowledge except:

- You have some basic programming experience.
- You know how to create a web application.
- You know how to use the command line.
- You can use a text editor on a console.

We also assume you are familar with basic Linux or Windows shell commands, and how to install additional software to your computer.

The software you install will provide you with a complete working OpenShift environment that you can use locally for development or testing.

We have used Java and the WildFly application server for the examples in this book. You do not need to be proficient in Java. If you are familar with any of the popular programming languages you will do just fine.

Why We Wrote This Book

We want to enable you to become self-sufficient in the basic use of OpenShift for creating and hosting your web applications, in as few words as possible. Therefore, we will not go into long explanations of the technologies used in OpenShift or different programming paradigms, but instead will give you links where you can go to read more.

Navigating This Book

The aim of this book is to get you up and running on OpenShift as quickly as possible. To that end, we dive into the most crucial content first and fill in the finer details as we go along.

- Chapters 1 and 2 provide a basic introduction to a container application platform, as well as the basic terms and technologies you will need to understand for the rest of the book.
- Chapter 3 provides instructions on how you can install a self contained version of the OpenShift environment on your own computer.
- Chapter 4 steps you through deploying your first application to OpenShift.

- Chapter 5 adds in a database to the application, providing it with a way of managing application data.

- Chapter 6 delves into managing deployments of your application and how to scale it up to handle more users.

- Chapter 7 introduces application templates, a means of simplifying new application deployments.

- Chapter 8 covers basic management commands for working with and understanding what your application is doing.

- Chapter 9 discusses deploying your own Docker images to OpenShift.

Online Resources

In this book you will install a self contained OpenShift environment based on OpenShift Origin (*https://www.openshift.org*). This is the upstream Open Source version of OpenShift that Red Hat's OpenShift Enterprise (*https://www.openshift.com/enterprise/*), OpenShift Dedicated (*https://www.openshift.com/dedicated/*) and OpenShift Online (*https://www.openshift.com*) products are based on. The all-in-one virtual machine used is available from the OpenShift Origin site (*https://www.openshift.org/vm/*).

OpenShift Origin will always include all the latest features, with support being provided by the OpenShift community.

The OpenShift product releases are created as a regular snapshot of the OpenShift Origin project. The product releases do not always have the very latest features, but if you have a commercial Red Hat subscription, the product releases include support from Red Hat.

If you would like to try out the OpenShift Enterprise version, a couple of options are available.

The first is to sign up to the Red Hat developers program at Red Hat Developers page (*http://developers.redhat.com*).

This is a free program and allows you to access versions of Red Hat products for personal use on your own computer. One of the products made available through the program is the Red Hat Container Development Kit (*http://developers.redhat.com/products/cdk/overview/*).

This includes a version of OpenShift that you can install on your own computer, but which is based on OpenShift Enterprise rather than OpenShift Origin.

A second way of trying out OpenShift Enterprise is via the Amazon Web Services (AWS) Test Drive program (*https://aws.amazon.com/testdrive/redhat/*).

This will set you up an OpenShift environment running across a multi node cluster on AWS.

Take a look at more in-depth documentation on OpenShift and how to use it at the OpenShift documentation site (*https://docs.openshift.org*).

Check out the OpenShift blog (*https://blog.openshift.com*), where regular articles are published on OpenShift.

Want to hear about how others in the OpenShift community are using OpenShift, or wish to share your own experiences, you can join the OpenShift Commons (*http://commons.openshift.org*).

If you have questions or issues, you can reach the OpenShift team through Stack Overflow (*http://stackoverflow.com*), via email to *openshift@redhat.com*, on Twitter (@openshift), or in the #openshift channel on IRC's FreeNode network.

Conventions Used in This Book

The following typographical conventions are used in this book:

Italic
: Indicates new terms, URLs, email addresses, filenames, and file extensions.

`Constant width`
: Used for program listings, as well as within paragraphs to refer to program elements such as variable or function names, databases, data types, environment variables, statements, and keywords.

`Constant width bold`
: Shows commands or other text that should be typed literally by the user.

`Constant width italic`
: Shows text that should be replaced with user-supplied values or by values determined by context.

 This icon signifies a tip, suggestion, or general note.

 This icon indicates a warning or caution.

Using Code Examples

Supplemental material (code examples, exercises, etc.) is available for download at *https://github.com/gshipley/book-insultapp*.

This book is here to help you get your job done. In general, if example code is offered with this book, you may use it in your programs and documentation. You do not need to contact us for permission unless you're reproducing a significant portion of the code. For example, writing a program that uses several chunks of code from this book does not require permission. Selling or distributing a CD-ROM of examples from O'Reilly books does require permission. Answering a question by citing this book and quoting example code does not require permission. Incorporating a significant amount of example code from this book into your product's documentation does require permission.

We appreciate, but do not require, attribution. An attribution usually includes the title, author, publisher, and ISBN. For example: "*OpenShift for Developers* by Grant Shipley and Graham Dumpleton (O'Reilly). Copyright 2016 Rad Hat, Inc., 978-1-491-94300-7."

If you feel your use of code examples falls outside fair use or the permission given above, feel free to contact us at permissions@oreilly.com.

Safari® Books Online

 Safari Books Online is an on-demand digital library that delivers expert content in both book and video form from the world's leading authors in technology and business.

Technology professionals, software developers, web designers, and business and creative professionals use Safari Books Online as their primary resource for research, problem solving, learning, and certification training.

Safari Books Online offers a range of product mixes and pricing programs for organizations, government agencies, and individuals. Subscribers have access to thousands of books, training videos, and prepublication manuscripts in one fully searchable database from publishers like O'Reilly Media, Prentice Hall Professional, Addison-Wesley Professional, Microsoft Press, Sams, Que, Peachpit Press, Focal Press, Cisco Press, John Wiley & Sons, Syngress, Morgan Kaufmann, IBM Redbooks, Packt, Adobe Press, FT Press, Apress, Manning, New Riders, McGraw-Hill, Jones & Bartlett, Course Technology, and dozens more. For more information about Safari Books Online, please visit us online.

How to Contact Us

Please address comments and questions concerning this book to the publisher:

O'Reilly Media, Inc.
1005 Gravenstein Highway North
Sebastopol, CA 95472
800-998-9938 (in the United States or Canada)
707-829-0515 (international or local)
707-829-0104 (fax)

To comment or ask technical questions about this book, send email to bookquestions@oreilly.com.

For more information about our books, courses, conferences, and news, see our website at *http://www.oreilly.com*.

Find us on Facebook: *http://facebook.com/oreilly*

Follow us on Twitter: *http://twitter.com/oreillymedia*

Watch us on YouTube: *http://www.youtube.com/oreillymedia*

Acknowledgments

Grant

Writing a book of any length takes a considerable amount of time. This is time that is most often stolen from my family. For that reason, I would like to thank my wonderful wife Leah and our four children—Jackson, Emily, Gavin, and Mason. Without their support and understanding, I would not have been able to create this book. I love you all very much.

I would also like to thank the entire OpenShift team at Red Hat, but especially the individuals who work directly on my team: Diane, Graham, Steve, Ryan, Jorge, and Marek. Working with such a fine group of folks makes this job not seem like a job at all and more about fun and pushing new technologies to the limit.

Other people I would like to thank, in no particular order, are as follows: Ashesh, Matt, Joe, Mike, Jake, Shawn, Sathish, Sam, Corey, Clayton, Dan, Thomas, Keck, Burr, Jakub, Miciah, and everyone else who has made OpenShift such a success. Lastly, I would like to thank Alexa Overbay for her dedication to the project and all of the hard work she puts in to help myself and the OpenShift team stay organized and running smoothly.

Graham

I would like to thank Grant and Red Hat for giving me the opportunity to work at a company which values and contributes to Open Source projects. I am a strong believer in Open Source and the good that it can create in the wider community. Through my own projects I have been attempting to improve the options available to Python developers for hosting web applications. I see the OpenShift project as being a very important part of that story and am thankful for the opportunity to work on it. With a family, my wife Wendy and two young children Kara and Caiden, the flexibility of being able to work remotely from home in my role with Red Hat has helped immensely in managing the day to day demands of children working their way through school. It does mean I often work strange hours and occasionally need to travel, but I have a family which is more than tolerant and is supportive of me, for which I am very grateful.

CHAPTER 1

Introduction to a Container Application Platform

In the few years since the original version of OpenShift was released, the cloud ecosystem has expanded at a rapid pace. New technologies and systems are springing up almost overnight. The new version of OpenShift (version 3) includes other technologies at the core of the platform, and it's worth it to spend some time learning about them and how to incorporate them into your development work. The core technology used as the basis of OpenShift includes Docker-based containers and orchestration via the Kubernetes system. Given that the core of the platform is based on containers, we often refer to OpenShift as a container application platform in that it is a platform designed for the development and deployment of containers.

So why did the OpenShift team rewrite their perfectly good PaaS (OpenShift 2)? The core architecture of OpenShift was built a bit over 4 years ago, which in the cloud evolution years (like dog years) is about 28 years ago, and a lot has changed since then. One example is Docker, which we discuss later in this chapter. The beginnings of the Docker project that you know today started as a container implementation using cgroups and kernel namespaces at a PaaS company named dotCloud. In March of 2013, the Docker project was released as an open source project and in July 2013, the company behind dotCloud pivoted and announced that their primary focus going forward would be the Docker container technology. OpenShift has been using containers since the beginning but the OpenShift team saw great potential within the Docker ecosystem—i.e., its potential as a "standard" for packaging applications, thereby creating better portability across environments.

The landscape in the cloud area has also been changing rapidly. The OpenShift team has four years of experience running one of the largest public PaaS systems and a large and successful install base of the on-premise enterprise version. The OpenShift team realized the time was right to use our knowledge, industry advancements, and new FOSS cloud projects to create an even better platform, which has been released as the OpenShift 3 container application platform.

Docker

Unless you have been living under a rock last two years, you have certainly heard about Docker and probably even heard about how Docker-based containers can solve all of your problems. While it is true that Docker-based containers are certainly cool, we need to be realistic about what this great technology provides and what it doesn't. In its simplest form, Docker provides users with a lightweight portable format that can be used to ship images of an application around to different environments. It accomplishes this while also packaging up all of the dependencies at both the system and application level to ensure the application runs as expected when deployed.

While Docker provides a great portable container format to ship applications around, it is important to remember that using Docker-based containers is just a small piece in the overall deployment puzzle that many organizations and individual developers face. A single Docker container that contains your application code is pretty trivial to get started with but once you move past the single container phase for your application, things become complex quickly, often leaving the developer to understand operational tasks instead of focusing on code. You may be thinking, "What on earth is he talking about?" For starters, things like:

- Load balancing a set of containers with or without session affinity
- Mounting persistent storage inside of the containers
- Placement and scheduling of containers on the infrastructure
- Rolling deployments and other operational considerations that traditional developers are not experts on

As you can see, things get complicated quickly when moving from a single development container to a real production application.

Given that Docker-based containers are such an important piece of the puzzle in a container application platform, Red Hat and the OpenShift team have spent a tremendous amount of engineering effort working on and with the Docker upstream project. In fact, at the time of writing, Red Hat is the second largest contributor to the project.

Kubernetes to the Rescue?

While Docker gets us a portable lightweight runtime, it lacks features for supporting n-tier applications. The OpenShift team understood this early on in the research phase when planning the new platform. We searched high and low for a great orchestration and scheduling system and made an early bet on the Kubernetes project Google started, and are now seeing great benefits as a result of that decision. Let's talk a little bit more about the Kubernetes project as you may not be familiar with it.

Kubernetes is a free and open source project started by Google in 2014. The first version was released in July 2015. The project is based off the Borg project, the technology Google uses to run containers at scale internally, launching over 7000 containers per second. When it came time to build their next version of the software they decided to open source the effort and Kubernetes was born.

Red Hat and the OpenShift team were key contributors to Kubernetes because of the value we see in the project to help with the scheduling, orchestration, and running of Docker-based containers for production workloads.

Again, just to be clear, both Docker and Kubernetes are great. However, they are just two pieces of the container application platform puzzle.

OpenShift

After all this goodness with Docker and Kubernetes, you are probably wondering where OpenShift fits in to the overall puzzle and what piece the platform provides. It turns out that Kubernetes is excellent at orchestrating and scheduling containers, but to have a platform that helps developers and sys admins deal with the piece most important to their "customers"—the application—something more is needed. The goal of OpenShift is to provide the best experience for developers and sysadmins developing, deploying, and running applications. In other words, OpenShift is a layer on top of Docker and Kubernetes that makes it accessible and easy for the developer to create applications and a platform that is a dream for operators to deploy containers on for both development and production workloads.

We are going to quickly cover some of the features OpenShift brings to the table to help developers (since that is the focus of this book) and then we will explore these more in depth throughout the book.

Web-Based Console

The OpenShift platform ships with a feature-rich web console that allows developers to perform the actions needed to deploy and run existing source code projects. For example, one of the features (as shown in Figure 1-1), is a graphical representation of an application that consists of multiple containers all load balanced, while also using a database as the backend storage engine.

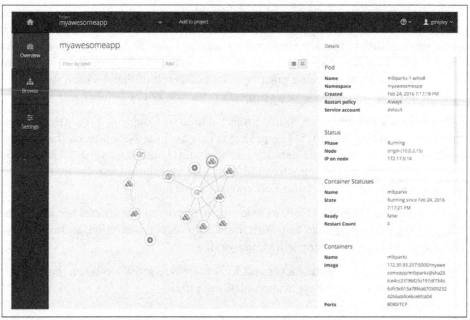

Figure 1-1. OpenShift resource visualization

Other tasks a developer would normally perform via the web console is scaling the application containers, creating projects, viewing log files, viewing the memory and CPU utilization of a container, and other common functions. The web console is a great tool as it provides a single interface for all aspects of your development project.

Command-Line Tool

OpenShift also provides a command-line tool that is written in the Go programming language. This tool, called *oc*, is a single binary executable provided for all major operating systems including Microsoft Windows, Apple OS X, and Linux. If you enjoy working on the command line, the *oc* tool is a first-class citizen and can be used to perform any operation that can be accomplished via the web console. The greatest benefit of using the oc command-line tool is that you have a single executable to perform all operations instead of having to interface directly with multiple tools such as the ones provides with Docker and Kubernetes. You can think of it as "one tool to rule them all." Okay, that may be a bad LOTR reference, I know.

Source-to-Image

The true power of OpenShift comes in with the S2I (Source-to-Image) open source project that the OpenShift Team created as part of the OpenShift platform. The team knows that developers want to take advantage of all of the benefits that running applications in containers provides, but don't want to spend their day creating Dockerfiles or running Docker builds while also having to do all of the orchestration by hand.

In its simplest form, the S2I-based Docker images allow developers to interact with the platform from a pure source code perspective. What this means is that OpenShift only needs to know the URL of your git repository and then the platform takes care of the rest. Under the covers, when you create a new project and container, the platform matches a base image of the desired runtime up with your source, performs a build, and then creates a new Docker image on the fly.

For a more concrete example, let's assume we have a Java-based project that uses the Maven build system. When using the WildFly application server and a git repository that contains your code, the platform will download the base WildFly image, clone your repo, identify it as a Maven project, run a Maven build, and take the artifact of that build and create a new Docker image that contains both the WildFly runtime and your build artifact. Finally, it will deploy the build artifact and then start up the resulting container. I know this may sound complicated, but don't worry, the platform takes care of all of the heavy lifting. We will dive into more detail as we progress through the book.

Integrated Logging and Metrics

One of the most important aspects of any software development project is the ability to troubleshoot issues as they arise. Since the beginning of time, one of the first places a developer looks when beginning the debug process is the application logs for the project. OpenShift provides a comprehensive view of your application logs including runtime logs, build logs, and deployment logs. Having these at your fingertips through the web console and *oc* tool greatly simplifies the troubleshooting process when using containers.

Another important aspect is metrics about your applications, utilization of system resources. The OpenShift platform includes support for this as shown in Figure 1-2, which details the memory and CPU utilization for a container running a Java application server and accompanying application.

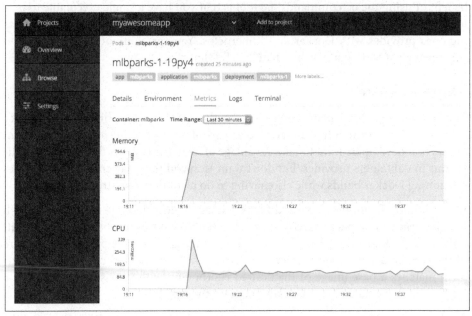

Figure 1-2. OpenShift metrics viewer

Summary

In this chapter we learned about the OpenShift container application platform and the benefits it adds for developers on top of plain old Docker and Kubernetes. There are certainly more advantages to using a full platform than what we have briefly discussed in this chapter. Never fear, as we progress through the contents of this book, we explore more topics in detail to ensure you are successful as a developer using OpenShift.

CHAPTER 2

Concepts You Need to Understand

Now that you understand the bigger picture of where we are going with Docker containers, Kubernetes, and OpenShift, we need to introduce you to some of the key terminology we will use throughout the book.

We cover the basic concepts of Kubernetes and discuss how OpenShift builds on them. In general, you can view Kubernetes as being aimed at Ops teams, providing them with a tool for running containers at scale in production. OpenShift adds to this by also supporting the work of a Dev team and others by making the job of the Ops team easier, which helps to bridge the gap between Dev and Ops and thus enable the latest DevOps philosophy.

Interacting with OpenShift

The primary grouping concept in Kubernetes is the *namespace*. Namespaces, as the term suggests, provide a scope for names. More specifically, namespaces provide the scope named resources that describe your application and how it should be deployed. Namespaces are also a way to divide cluster resources between multiple uses. That being said, there is no security between namespaces in Kubernetes; if you are a "user" in a Kubernetes cluster, you can see all the different namespaces and the resources defined in them.

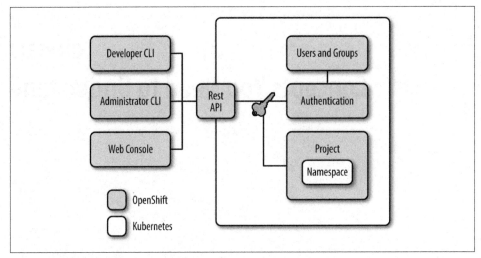

Figure 2-1. OpenShift access and control

The first new concept OpenShift adds is *project*, which effectively wraps a namespace, with access to the namespace being controlled via the project. Access is controlled through an authentication and authorization model based on *users* and *groups*. Projects in OpenShift therefore provide the walls between namespaces, ensuring that users, or applications, can only see and access what they are allowed to.

This enables multitenant use of an OpenShift cluster with access privileges determined by the identity of the user or the team they belong to. Users can be assigned to multiple groups and can inherit permissions depending on group membership. Groups often map to teams or functional units within a company, such as developers, QA, or production.

OpenShift provides a number of different ways to interact with an OpenShift cluster. The OpenShift command-line tool oc is the primary way most users interact with OpenShift. The command-line tool talks via a REST API exposed by the OpenShift cluster. We cover installation of the command-line tool in the next chapter.

If you want to avoid using the command line tool, or you want to automate your interactions with the OpenShift cluster, you can always use the REST API directly. Diving into the API is beyond the scope of this book, but we wanted to make sure you know there is an API, since it can be useful when integrating with an existing external system for continuous integration and deployment (CI/CD). You can find documentation on the REST API at OpenShift's documentation page (*http://red.ht/ 1WKU0J6*).

Finally, OpenShift includes a web console. This provides a web-based GUI for those who would prefer not to use command-line tools. For some tasks, such as the initial deployment of an application, the web console presents a more user-friendly forms-driven interface based on application templates, which can help you get going quicker. We will be using both the command line and the web console throughout the book.

If you are familiar with Kubernetes you may also know of the command-line tool kubectl. In OpenShift this would normally only be used in the setup and internal management of the cluster. Since it is more of an administration tool in the context of OpenShift we will not be discussing it here.

The Deployed Application

You may be wondering: "Is a namespace the same thing as an application?" OpenShift has no formal concept of an application, thereby allowing an application to be flexible depending on a user's needs.

You can dedicate one to everything related to just one application. Or, so long as you label all the resources making up an application so you know what goes with what, you can also use the namespace to hold more than one.

What are the different parts that go into making up an application? That is what we will cover now.

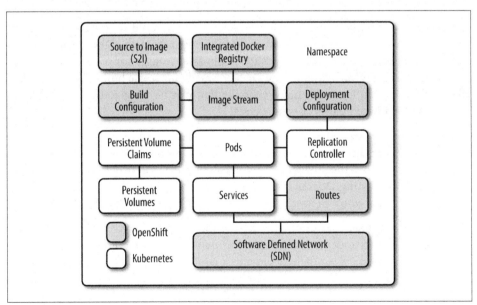

Figure 2-2. OpenShift project (Namespace)

The most basic unit in OpenShift are *pods*. A pod is one or more *containers* guaranteed to be running on the same host. The containers within a pod share a unique IP address. They can communicate with each other via the "localhost" and also all share any *volumes* (persistent storage). The containers themselves are started from an *image*, which in our case is a Docker image.

When scaled up, an application will have more than one copy of itself, and each copy will have its own local state. Each copy corresponds to a different instance of a pod with the pods being managed by the *replication controller*. As each pod has a unique IP, we need an easy way to address the set of all pods as a whole. This is where a *service* comes into play. The service gets its own IP and a DNS name. When making a connection to a service, OpenShift will automatically route the connection to one of the pods associated with that service.

Although a service has a DNS name, it is still only accessible within the OpenShift cluster and is not accessible externally. To make a service externally accessible, a *route* needs to be created. Creating a route automatically sets up haproxy or a hardware-based router, with an externally addressable DNS name, exposing the service and load-balancing inbound traffic across the pods.

Build and Deployment Process

Getting your application running and managed for you is all well and good, but we need a way of getting the application built and deployed in the first place.

The *build configuration* contains a description of how to build source code and a base image into a new image—the primary method for delivering changes to your application. Builds can be source based and use S2I builder images for common languages like Java, PHP, Ruby, or Python, or be Docker based and create builds from a Dockerfile. Each build configuration has webhooks that can be triggered automatically by changes to their base images or source code.

The output of the build process is an image, which is stored in an integrated Docker registry ready for distribution out to nodes when the application is deployed. The *image stream* is how the image and its versions are tracked by OpenShift. If you already have an existing Docker image on an external registry such as Docker Hub, it can also be referenced by an image stream instead of building it locally.

When deploying an application, the *deployment configuration* is what defines the template for a pod and manages deploying new images or configuration changes whenever those change. A single deployment configuration is usually analogous to a single microservice. A deployment configuration supports a number of different deployment strategies including a complete shutdown then restart, rolling updates, or your own fully customized behaviors. Different strategies support *pre*, *mid*, and *post* hooks, allowing you to perform specific actions at key points of a deployment. The result of a deployment is the replication controller, which then manages your pods and keeps them running.

As you can see, various parts go together to define your application and the build process to create it. But OpenShift manages the creation of all of the parts when using the web console or the command-line tools. If you do need to implement a more customized configuration, you can still jump in and change the configuration and create your own templates to automate future builds and configurations using your customizations.

Online Cheat Sheet

When you move beyond the book and start using OpenShift in your day-to-day activities (development and operations), use the handy online cheat sheet available by running the oc types command. It gives you a quick summary of the different conceptual types and definitions used in OpenShift like those we covered here:

```
$ oc types
Concepts and Types

Kubernetes and OpenShift help developers and operators build, test, and deploy
applications in a containerized cloud environment. Applications may be composed
of all of the components below, although most developers will be concerned with
Services, Deployments, and Builds for delivering changes.

Concepts:

* Containers:
    A definition of how to run one or more processes inside of a portable Linux
    environment. Containers are started from an Image and are usually isolated
    from other containers on the same machine.

...
```

Also make use of the oc help command and the --help option to see descriptions and examples and learn how to use the command in question.

Summary

In this chapter, we covered key terminology you need to understand, and we explained which of those concepts originate in Kubernetes versus OpenShift. In the next chapter, we will describe how you can install the OpenShift software on your system.

CHAPTER 3

Installing the All-in-One VM

For the exercises in this book we will be using a virtual machine (VM) that has all the pieces of an OpenShift server already installed and configured. This machine will be routable from your local system so you can treat it like a hosted version of OpenShift and can view the URLs you create.

This image is based off of OpenShift Origin (*https://github.com/openshift/origin*) and is a fully functioning OpenShift instance with an integrated Docker registry. The aim of this project is to allow web developers and other interested parties to run Open-Shift V3 on their own computer. The VM is configured by default to have a separate IP address (10.2.2.2) from your local machine, and it includes a network configuration that assigns each new container deployed on the platform its own unique IP address. This gives the illusion that the VM is running on separate hardware in a data center or public cloud while in fact it's running locally on your machine.

The OpenShift master, node, Docker registry, and other pieces run on one VM. Given its focus on application developers, it should NOT be used in production. While the Vagrantfile only specifies 2 gigs of RAM, you can edit the file to increase this setting if you want to run more containers concurrently in your instance.

The VM uses xip.io (*https://xip.io*) to provide DNS resolution with application URLs. The advantage of this is that you actually get routable URLs to your local machine without browser or Vagrant plug-ins that may not work on your machine. The draw-back is that you need to be online whenever you use the VM and xip.io may be blocked by your company's firewalls. We apologize in advance if this happens. Our only suggestion is to either try to work on a different network, talk to your admin about opening up xip.io, or try the Landrush plug-in (*https://github.com/phinze/land rush*) for Vagrant.

Since we wanted developers to be able to use any Docker image they want, we had to turn off some security in OpenShift. By default, OpenShift will not allow a container to run as root or even a nonrandom container assigned userid. Most Docker images in the Dockerhub do not follow this best practice and instead run as root. Furthermore, a large majority of Dockerhub images are not patched for well-known vulnerabilities. Therefore, use images from Docker Hub with caution. We think some of the risk is mitigated because you are running OpenShift in a VM, but still—be careful about which Docker images you run.

While we will go through the install instructions here, the latest install instructions and information can be found on the OpenShift.org VM page (*https://openshift.org/vm*).

Software Requirements

You only need a couple of things on your system to run the all-in-one image: Vagrant, VirtualBox, and the oc command-line tool.

Install VirtualBox

The OpenShift all-in-one image uses the VirtualBox as the virtualization system. You are probably wondering why we chose VirtualBox instead of other tools. We chose it for the following reasons:

- It is cross-platform, allowing Mac, Windows, and Linux users use it.
- It is free and open source, allowing everyone freedom as in beer and as in speech when choosing the virtualization tool.

Download the correct package for your operating system from the VirtualBox download page (*https://www.virtualbox.org/wiki/Downloads*).

Once you have it downloaded, follow the instructions on the VirtualBox site to install the software.

Install Vagrant

Vagrant is a software tool that allows users to create and configure lightweight, reproducible, and portable development environments. It works in conjunction with virtualization (both VMs and IaaS) to automate all the steps necessary to get your dev environment going. You probably already have Vagrant installed on your system, but if you don't simply head over to the download page (*https://www.vagrantup.com/downloads.html*) and follow the instructions for your operating system.

For Linux systems, is it recommended that you install via the package manager provided by your distribution. For example, to install Vagrant on Fedora 23, issue the following command:

```
$ sudo dnf install vagrant
```

Vagrant init

The last thing we need to download is the Vagrantfile (*https://www.openshift.org/vm/Vagrantfile*), which tells Vagrant what type of system we want to download as well as some configuration information.

Change Your Memory Configuration

The last thing you may want to do is customize the amount of memory that you want the OpenShift container application platform to use. By default, the Vagrantfile will allocate 4 GB of memory for the platform, but you may want to change this depending on your specific needs. For example, my development rig has 32 GB of memory (yeah, I am bragging a bit here) so I like to allocate 16 GB. The relevant line you want to change in the Vagrantfile is:

```
vb.memory = "4096"
```

Start Things Up

The last thing we need to do is start up the platform. To do this, ensure you are in the directory where your Vagrantfile is located and issue the following command:

```
$ vagrant up --provider=virtualbox
```

BAM!

At this point, the all-in-one image will be downloaded so be patient as it depends on your Internet connection.

Download the Latest oc Command-Line Tool

OpenShift 3 allows you to work from the command line, web console, or via the Eclipse IDE using the latest JBoss tools. However, we are going to focus on using the command-line tool and the web console here. The oc tool is a single executable that is written in the Go programming language. For this reason, there is actually nothing to install. You simply need to download the tool and add it to your PATH. Sounds easy, right? Well, it is for OS X and Linux users, but Windows users will need to hunt around a bit to change the system path. Let's start with downloading the toolset. The only real requirement for the oc tool is that you are using a 64-bit operating system. The VM instruction (*https://openshift.org/vm*) page has links to the appropriate version of the oc command-line tool based on the version of the VM you are using.

Once you have the tool downloaded, extract the contents and add the oc executable to your PATH. For example, if I extracted the contents to the cli directory in my home directory, I would issue the following command in both Linux and OS X:

```
$ export PATH=$PATH:~/cli/
```

Windows

Changing your PATH in Windows varies by OS version but the general workflow is to right-click your computer name inside of File Explorer, and select Advanced system settings (I guess changing your PATH is considered an advanced task?)

Click the Advanced tab and then click Environment variables. Once the new dialog opens, select the Path variable and add ";C:\CLI" at the end (ensure you replace C:\CLI with the location of where you extracted the tool). You could also just copy it to C:\Windows or a directory you know is already on your path. For more detailed instructions, by operating system:

- Windows XP (*https://support.microsoft.com/en-us/kb/310519*)
- Windows Vista (*http://bit.ly/1ZhXZvQ*)
- Windows 7 (*http://bit.ly/1ZhXSjM*)
- Windows 8 (*http://bit.ly/1ZhXUZ6*)
- Windows 10: Follow the directions above.

Initial Login from the Web Console

Now that we have everything in place let's go ahead and log in as the admin on the box so we can do one last preparatory step. The VM has no set users and passwords so you can create your usernames and passwords as you go along:

1. Go to the web console for your OpenShift instance: *https://10.2.2.2:8443*.

2. At the login prompt type **admin** for the user and **password** for the password, as shown in Figure 3-1.

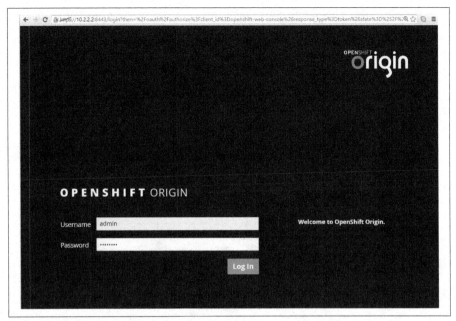

Figure 3-1. Use admin for the username and password for the password when prompted

3. You should see a screen listing all the projects available to the admin user. We will discuss some of these projects later in the book, but for now, click the *openshift-infra* project, as shown in Figure 3-2.

Figure 3-2. Select the openshift-infra project

4. Inside this project you will see a service and a route:

hawkular-metrics.apps.10.2.2.2.xip.io   (*https://hawkular-metrics.apps.*
10.2.2.2.xip.io)

Go ahead and click that link. If you get a browser warning go ahead and accept
the certificate.

5. Now we can go ahead and log out as admin and log in as a user without the clut-
tered project view (see Figure 3-3).

Figure 3-3. Log out of the admin account

Now Log In from the Command Line

Let's go ahead and log in as a normal user using the command-line tools:

```
$ oc login https://10.2.2.2:8443

Authentication required for https://10.2.2.2:8443 (openshift)
Username: user
Password: password
Login successful.

You don't have any projects. You can try to create a new project, by running

    $ oc new-project <projectname>
```

As noted earlier, you can create any username and password; we use *user:password* in
our examples. For now, do not create a new project; we will do this in the next chapter.

In Windows, the command-line tool will not let you log in due to
the self-signed certificate for the server. You need to log in passing
a flag to tell the command-line tools to ignore the self-signed cert:

```
oc login https://10.2.2.2:8443
--insecure-skip-tls-verify=true
```

Now Log In to the Web Console as a Normal User

Now let's bring the experience full circle by logging in as the same user in the web
console. You already logged in on the web console a couple of steps above, so just do

the same thing except use the normal username and password we used previously. You should see a screen like this the one in Figure 3-4.

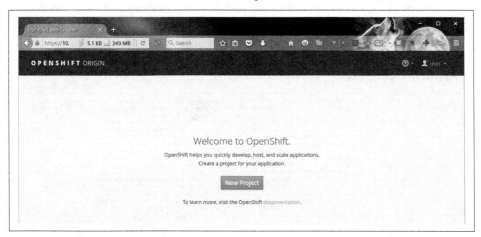

Figure 3-4. OpenShift welcome screen

Again, we're not going to create a project right now. On to our final step.

Create a GitHub Account

Finally, to make things easier here in terms of code and exchanging ideas, you need to sign up for a GitHub (*https://github.com*) account. You will use this to fork code and to make it easier to builds in OpenShift. If you don't already have an account go ahead and create one (see Figure 3-5).

Figure 3-5. Create an account if you don't have one

GitHub supports using two-factor authentication (TFA) for your account and we strongly recommend you use it. TFA means that in addition to your normal password, a second factor is required to log in (usually a random code generated every minute or so on your phone). We have had two different online accounts saved from being hacked by using TFA. To turn on TFA, go to your settings (the icon at the top-right of your GitHub page, go to Security, and then turn on two-factor authentication, as shown in Figure 3-6.

Figure 3-6. Turn on two-factor authentication

The system will walk you through a few steps to enable it. While it may seem like a bit of a hassle, you will thank us someday (or not because you never notice *not* being hacked).

Summary

In this chapter, we set up your local machine so you have a working instance of OpenShift running and ready to interact with. You also got a chance to log in, do some easy configuration, and finally set up a GitHub account for your code. At this point you are probably thinking, "When do I actually get to work on code?!?" Well, the time has come—from now it is all hands-on development work with OpenShift.

CHAPTER 4

Developing and Deploying Your First Application

At this point, you should have a good understanding of the OpenShift platform and have it running locally. Now comes the good stuff, actually using the platform for application development and deployment. In this chapter, we are going to create and deploy our first application using the popular open source WildFly application server for Java-based applications. We will also use a bit of git, since it is the main way OpenShift interacts with source code. But before we get started, we need to cover a few basics of both Git and WildFly in case you are not familiar with them.

Understanding the Tools

Git

Git (*http://git-scm.com/*) is a program that provides distributed version control. You may have used Subversion, CVS, or Visual SourceSafe, which are all centralized version control systems. In centralized systems there is a master server and everyone else has a copy of the code that they need to synchronize with the master. With Git, every repository, from the one on your laptop to the one on a remote server, is considered a legitimate master. Everything is kept in sync through patches sent between repositories. You can use Git as a pseudo-centralized version control system by having everyone on the team agree on "the master." Wikipedia has a good discussion (*http://bit.ly/ 1Zign7I*) about some of the differences between centralized and distributed version control systems.

The important thing to keep in mind about Git is that the Git repository on your machine is considered a repository, and you need to commit your changes there first.

That means you have to add any new files and commit any changes on your local machine before you can push your changes to any other Git repository.

On OpenShift, in order to take advantage of the S2I builder images, you will need to have your source code in a reachable Git repository. By reachable, we mean that your OpenShift server has the ability to see the repository and clone contents over the network. This can include both public and private repositories as long as OpenShift can establish a network connection to the Git repository host. For the work we do here, you will have two Git repositories:

- A remote repository on GitHub (or any public Git repository of your choice)
- A local repository on your local machine

There are three basic commands you need to work with OpenShift:

git add
> Add a file to your local Git repository. Even if you have a file in the directory representing your Git repo, it is *not* considered part of the repository until you add it.

git commit
> Commit any changes you have made to your local repository.

git push
> Push the changes from your local repository up to your publicly addressable repository on GitHub.

If you are interested in learning more, you're in luck; there are several different (*http://bit.ly/1dubZuh*) decent documents (*http://bit.ly/1mjkIaS*) to get you going (*http://bit.ly/1r0Je1h*). If you are coming from Subversion land, there is even a Git introduction for you (*http://bit.ly/1gLk81Y*). The fine people at GitHub have also put together a nice collection of resources about Git (*http://bit.ly/O86g76*).

A quick note about the difference between Git and GitHub (*https://github.com*). Git is the tool, and GitHub is a site that allows for public and private hosting of Git repositories. GitHub also adds a lot of social features, making it very easy for developers to find and collaborate on code. That said, you can certainly use GitHub with OpenShift while using the automated builder images provided with S2I.

WildFly

If you are a Java Developer, you are probably familiar with the WildFly application server from Red Hat. If not, what you need to know is that WildFly is an application server that implements the Java Platform, Enterprise Edition specification, often referred to as Java EE. What you may not know is that WildFly was formally known as JBoss AS and went through a name change in November of 2014. This was done to more closely align with the open source community the server is targeted at and to ensure developers were not confused between JBoss AS and JBoss EAP.

WildFly is a free and open source project under the LGPL version 2.1 license. For this book, we are going to be using version 10 of the WildFly application server that was released in February of 2016.

 We will be using the WildFly server for this example but the code will also work on the popular Tomcat server.

For more information on the WildFly application server, refer to the official website (*http://wildfly.org*).

If you are not a Java developer, don't fret, as you can still follow along with the exercises in this book as the main purpose is to learn how to interact with the platform. The process is almost identical regardless of the programming language or server your application project uses.

Creating Our First Application

Now that we understand the basic tools we need for our first application, Git and WildFly, it's time to dig in and start working with the platform. However, we do have to complete one additional step before we actually deploy our first application: we need to fork, or make a copy of, the sample application we will be using in this chapter.

Creating a Copy of the Sample Application

In Chapter 1, you created an account on the popular GitHub service. Now we are going to use that account to fork the application code that we will be using to deploy. As is often standard practice in technical books, the first application we are going to deploy is a simple *Hello, world* application. Let's get started.

Log in to your GitHub account and then point your browser to the repository for the sample application (*https://github.com/gshipley/book-helloworld*).

Once the page has loaded, and you are authenticated with your GitHub account, you should see a fork button in the upper righthand corner of the screen as shown in Figure 4-1.

Figure 4-1. Fork project

After you fork the application code, you will have a working copy in your account that you are free to modify and use for deployment on the platform.

Creating the Application

Now that we have a copy of the source code project in our personal GitHub account, we can create a project and a corresponding pod that will contain our deployed source code. The first thing we want to do is log in to the web console by opening up the following URL: *https://10.2.2.2:8443*.

When prompted for the username and password, use the following:

- **Username:** user
- **Password:** password

Next, click the *New Project* button, which will drop you in the projection creation flow as shown in Figure 4-2.

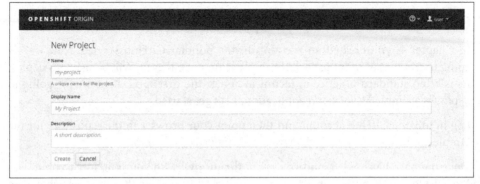

Figure 4-2. New project

Enter this information in the fields provided:

Field Name	What to enter	Description
Name	`wfproject`	The name of your project
Display Name	`WildFly Project`	The project name that will be displayed in the UI
Description	`Application using WildFly server`	Details about your project

 Project names have to be unique across the entire OpenShift environment. You can think of a project as a unique namespace for your applications.

After you fill in the fields above, click *Create*. You will then select the type of template you would like to use for your first application. For this example, click the *wildfly:10.0* application template. You will then name your application as well as the URL for your GitHub repository that we forked previously in this chapter, as shown in Figure 4-3.

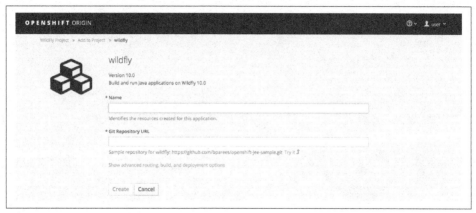

Figure 4-3. Select template

Enter **helloworld** as the name, and then paste the URL for your repository on GitHub. If you are not familiar with GitHub, the repository URL is shown on the repository home page as shown in Figure 4-4.

Figure 4-4. GitHub repo URL

Many first-time users of GitHub find that the repository URL is not the same URL displayed in the browser. A Git repository URL normally ends with the *.git* extension.

Once you have entered in the name and correct repository URL, click the *Create* button. Then watch the magic begin!

At this point, the process we discussed in Chapter 1 regarding S2I is executed. Depending on the speed of your Internet connection, this may take a few minutes as the builder image is downloaded and the source code for the project is compiled. You will know your source code is ready when the indicator for your pod turns blue as shown in Figure 4-5.

Figure 4-5. Running pod

Note that the application also has an associated route, which is the DNS name for your application on your local network. In this specific example, the URL is *helloworld-wfproject.apps.10.2.2.2.xip.io*. If you click that URL you will be directed to the running application and will see the following content on the displayed web page:

```
Hello, OpenShift.
```

Congratulations! You are now officially an expert at deploying Java-based projects using Docker-based containers. That wasn't so bad, was it?

Making a Code Change and Starting a New Build

In the previous section, we deployed a very simple application. It is also important to understand how to modify the code and begin a new build of your project.

If you don't have the project cloned locally to your machine, do that now. If you are not familiar with Git, you will want to execute the following command in the directory where you would like the source code to be stored ensuring you replace *your_repository_url* with the correct *.git* repo file you used to create the project:

```
git clone your_repository_url
```

To see how modifying code works with the platform, open up your favorite editor, or IDE, and edit the following file in the repository:

```
src/main/webapp/index.html
```

Find the following line:

```
<h1>Hello, OpenShift.</h1>
```

Change it to:

```
<h1>Hello, OpenShift builds.</h1>
```

Now that you have modified some super mission critical source code, it's time to commit the change to your local repository and then push the change to the remote repository on GitHub. To accomplish this, issue the following commands:

```
git commit -am "Updated index.html to change message."
git push
```

You can verify that the change was reflected in your upstream (GitHub) repository by visiting your project on the GitHub web console.

Now we need to start a new build of our application so OpenShift can deploy the new source. Go to the project overview page inside the OpenShift web console and then click *Browse* and then *Builds*. You will see a table listing each of the different types of builds that have been created for your project. At this point, you should only see one build with the following information:

Name	Last Build	Status	Created	Type	Source
helloworld	#1	Complete in one minute, 14 seconds	9 minutes ago	Source	repo URL

Note that the name of the build (*helloworld*) is actually a link. Click the name and you will be taken to the build overview page as shown in Figure 4-6.

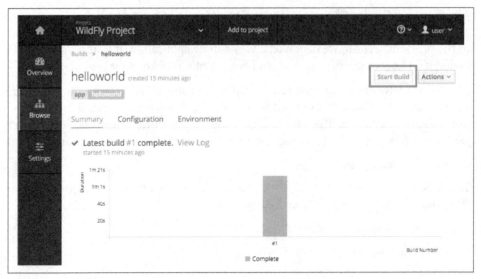

Figure 4-6. Build overview

Once you click the *Start Build* button, a new build will be triggered that will clone the updated source code from the application's GitHub repository and the remainder of the S2I flow will be executed. Once the build and deployment are complete, you will be able to see the result of the modifications by clicking the application's URL displayed on the project overview page in the web console. In this specific example, the URL is *helloworld-wfproject.apps.10.2.2.2.xip.io.*

Summary

In this chapter, we learned how to create and deploy our first application on the OpenShift platform. After we deployed the application, we learned how to make a code change and perform a new build. In the next chapter, we will continue working on the application by looking at adding dependencies for the language runtime as well connecting and using a database on the OpenShift platform.

CHAPTER 5

Adding Dependencies and a Database

In the last chapter, we deployed a very simple *Hello, world* application. In this chapter we are going to create a new application that contains a more real-world example. In the application we will be building here the user will be insulted with a friendly message. What could be more fun than that? How about a Elizabethan insult chosen randomly? These Shakespearean insult words have been floating around the Internet since before dial-up. Let's put them to good use complete with a database backend and a HTTP-based API. The insult consists of two adjectives and a noun and will look something like this:

```
Thou art a Mewling Motley-minded Vassal!
```

Let's get started.

Creating the Base Application

We are going to start simple by deploying a static version of the insult application that simply randomly chooses an insult and then displays it on a JSP page. In a previous chapter, you learned how to fork an application on GitHub. We are going to following those steps so we have a starting point for this application that we will then modify.

Forking the Repository and Deploying the Application

Point your favorite browser to the project's GitHub page (*https://github.com/gshipley/ book-insultapp*).

Once you have the repository open in your browser, fork the repository by clicking on the *Fork* button on the top righthand side of the screen. This will create a copy of the repository that you can modify.

After the project has been *forked* to your account, the next step is to create a new project to hold our application code and then deploy it using the WildFly application server. Let's start by creating a new project called *insultapp* using the following command:

```
oc new-project insultapp --display-name="Elizabethan Insult Application"
```

This command will create a new project for us called *insultapp* and will also be displayed in the WebUi with the display name we provided as shown Figure 5-1.

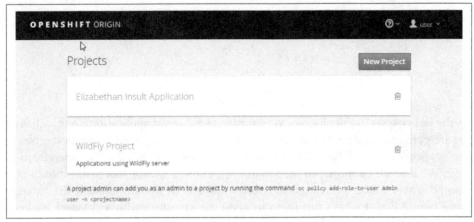

Figure 5-1. Project list

The next thing we need to do is create a deployment that contains our application code. We can do this with the *oc new-app* command while specifying the image we want to use as well as the repository we want to use for the build.

```
oc new-app wildfly:latest~https://github.com/gshipley/book-insultapp.git
--name='insults'
```

It is important to remember to use the repository URL for the version you forked and not the one shown in the example above.

You may be wondering what the tilde character in the *oc new-app* command means. When creating containers on the OpenShift platform it means you want to use an existing source code repository and take advantage of the S2I build process. After entering the preceding command, you will see the following output, which indicates the application deployment process has started:

```
--> Found image 330a039 (5 weeks old) in image stream "wildfly in project
    openshift" under tag :latest for "wildfly:latest"
    * A source build using source code from
    https://github.com/gshipley/book-insultapp.git will be
    created
      * The resulting image will be pushed to image stream
      "insults:latest"
```

```
* This image will be deployed in deployment config "insults"
* Port 8080/tcp will be load balanced by service "insults"
--> Creating resources with label app=insults ...
    ImageStream "insults" created
    BuildConfig "insults" created
    DeploymentConfig "insults" created
    Service "insults" created
--> Success
    Build scheduled for "insults" - use the logs command to track
    its progress.
    Run 'oc status' to view your app.
```

Testing the application

Once the Insult application has been deployed, the last thing we need to do is expose a route to the application and then verify that it is indeed serving up insults. To expose a route, issue the following command:

```
oc expose service insults
```

 One of the advantages of creating and deploying applications from the web console is that a route is automatically created for you. When deploying new containers while using the *oc* tool, you will need to expose the service manually.

Finally, we can verify that the application is working by visiting it via the exposed URL, which can be found in the web console or by running the following command:

```
oc get routes
```

The output will look like the following:

```
NAME     HOST/PORT                               PATH   SERVICE   LABELS
insults  insults-insultapp.apps.10.2.2.2.xip.io         insults   app=insults
```

What are you waiting for? Fire up your browser and get your first insult.

The code that generates the insults is pretty straightforward in that it just randomly chooses two adjectives and a noun from a multidimensional string array. This is shown in the following code, which can be found in the *InsultGenerator.java* file under the */src/main/java/org/openshift* directory:

```
package org.openshift;

import java.util.Random;

public class InsultGenerator {
    public String generateInsult() {
        String words[][] = {{"Artless", "Bawdy", "Beslubbering"},
        {"Base-court", "Bat-fowling", "Beef-witted"}, {"Apple-john",
        "Baggage", "Barnacle"}};
```

```
String vowels = "AEIOU";
String article = "an";
String firstAdjective = words[0][
new Random().nextInt(words[0].length)];
String secondAdjective = words[1][
new Random().nextInt(words[1].length)];
String noun = words[2][new Random().nextInt(words[2].length)];
if (vowels.indexOf(firstAdjective.charAt(0)) == -1) {
        article = "a";
}
return String.format("Thou art %s %s %s %s!", article,
firstAdjective, secondAdjective, noun);
    }
}
```

While the preceding code certainly works, we'd rather generate the insult using a longer list of words that is easily updated without having to change application code. For this reason, we are going to add the Postgres database to our application and then import a schema that contains more words to choose from.

The first thing we need to do is add our database to our project using the web console. Open up your browser and go to the *Elizabethan Insult Application* project we created. Once you are on the Overview page, click the *Add to project* button at the top of the screen as shown in Figure 5-2.

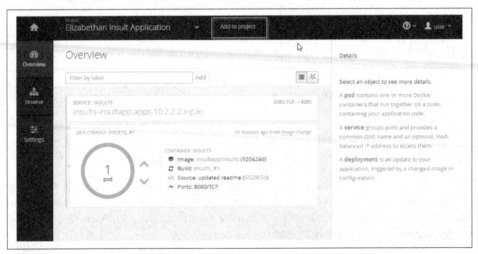

Figure 5-2. Add to project

On the next page that is displayed, type **postgres** in the filter box and select the *postgresql-persistent* image (see Figure 5-3).

Figure 5-3. Database selection

On the following page, you can specify configuration settings for your database such as the amount of disk storage to use, username and password values, and the default database name. For simplicity sake we are going to use the following values:

Field Name	What to enter	Description
Memory limit	512Mi	Since this is a small database, we only need 512 megabytes of memory.
Database service name	postgresql	The name of the resulting OpenShift service.
PostgreSQL user	insult	The username that has permission to use the database. If empty, it will be auto-generated.
PostgreSQL password	insult	The password for the user. If empty, it will be auto-generated.
PostgreSQL database name	insults	The name of the initial database that will be created.

Once you have provided the values in the above table, click the *Create* button to deploy a pod running your PostgreSQL container. Once the database has been created, your project overview page should list both your application code pod and your database pod, as shown in Figure 5-4.

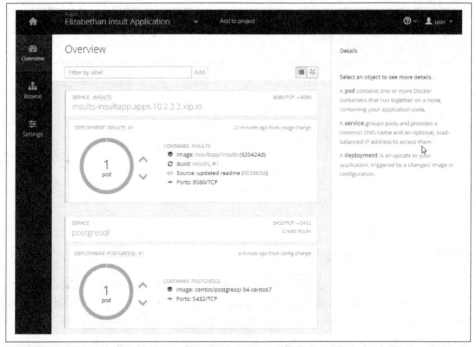

Figure 5-4. Project overview

One of the great features of the OpenShift platform is the ability to provide persistent volumes for your running pods. This ensures that data in your database doesn't suddenly disappear if the container is restarted. Another important aspect of persistent volumes is the ability to run both stateful and stateless applications on the platform. This is sometimes referred to as mode 1 and mode 2 applications as well as legacy and 12-factor applications.

Linking the database to the application

When we added the database, the platform stored all of the information needed to connect to the database as system environment variables initially only accessible to the database pods. The following variables were created in this example:

```
POSTGRESQL_PORT_5432_TCP_ADDR=172.30.76.249
POSTGRESQL_PORT=tcp://172.30.76.249:5432
POSTGRESQL_SERVICE_PORT_POSTGRESQL=5432
POSTGRESQL_PORT_5432_TCP=tcp://172.30.76.249:5432
POSTGRESQL_SERVICE_HOST=172.30.76.249
POSTGRESQL_DATABASE=insults
POSTGRESQL_PASSWORD=insult
POSTGRESQL_VERSION=9.4
POSTGRESQL_PORT_5432_TCP_PORT=5432
```

```
POSTGRESQL_SERVICE_PORT=5432
POSTGRESQL_PORT_5432_TCP_PROTO=tcp
POSTGRESQL_USER=insult
```

In order to be able to communicate to the database using these environment variables, we need to add them to DeploymentConfig for our insult application. Adding the environment variables to DeploymentConfig instead of directly in the running pod ensures that any new pod will be started with the variables it needs to connect. You could certainly just hard code these values in your application code but that is not a best practice! This can be done using the following command:

```
oc env dc insults -e POSTGRESQL_USER=insult  -e PGPASSWORD=insult
POSTGRESQL_DATABASE=insults
```

For the password you may notice that we used *PGPASSWORD* instead of *POSTGRESQL_USER_PASSWORD*. This is because the PostgreSQL database expects the password in this variable so you don't have to provide it when running *psql* on the command line, which we will just in just a few moments.

After you enter the above command, the "truth" of the application state will have changed, meaning that for a deployment to be considered valid, the running pod must contain those environment variables. This means a new rolling deployment will occur and your existing pod will be replaced with a new one. Pretty awesome stuff! You could have just as easily modified DeploymentConfig using the web console by editing the *.yaml* file directly. In order to modify *.yaml* files in the web console, browse to the deployment section and then click *Edit YAML* under the actions button.

Importing the database schema

At this point we have our application code deployed and a database running, but the database is empty so we need to fix that! In the source code repository for the application I have provided a file called *insults.sql* that contains all of the SQL needed to create our schema. An excerpt of the SQL is as follows:

```
DROP TABLE IF EXISTS short_adjective;
DROP TABLE IF EXISTS long_adjective;
DROP TABLE IF EXISTS noun;

BEGIN;

CREATE TABLE short_adjective (id serial PRIMARY KEY, string varchar);
CREATE TABLE long_adjective (id serial PRIMARY KEY, string varchar);
CREATE TABLE noun (id serial PRIMARY KEY, string varchar);

INSERT INTO short_adjective (string) VALUES ('artless');
INSERT INTO short_adjective (string) VALUES ('bawdy');
```

```
INSERT INTO short_adjective (string) VALUES ('beslubbering');
INSERT INTO short_adjective (string) VALUES ('bootless');
INSERT INTO short_adjective (string) VALUES ('churlish');
INSERT INTO short_adjective (string) VALUES ('cockered');
INSERT INTO short_adjective (string) VALUES ('clouted');
INSERT INTO short_adjective (string) VALUES ('craven');
```

We need to import the SQL to our database. We will use the *Terminal* application provided as part of the web console.

> If you don't like using the web console, you can also use the *oc rsh* command to open up a remote shell on the running container.

1. From the project overview screen, click the blue circle for your WildFly server (not your database) to list the pods that are currently running for your application, as shown in Figure 5-5.

Figure 5-5. Accessing the list of pods

2. After selecting the blue circle, you will then be shown a list of all the pods that are currently running. In this case, as shown in Figure 5-6, you will have only one pod running.

Figure 5-6. Pod list

3. Click the pod name and then click the *Terminal* button near the top of the screen, as shown in Figure 5-7.

Figure 5-7. Pod overview

This will open up a terminal session on the WildFly container that is running inside of the pod (Figure 5-8).

Figure 5-8. Pod terminal

4. Once you have the terminal open, you can import that schema with the following command:

```
psql -h $POSTGRESQL_SERVICE_HOST -p $POSTGRESQL_SERVICE_PORT \
    -U $POSTGRESQL_USER $POSTGRESQL_DATABASE < insults.sql
```

Bam! You now have several tables created inside of your database that contain a plethora of words to choose from to insult your users.

 When working with the terminal inside of the web console, I find it very useful to set my term type so that I have history and better usability for editing files. To do this, issue the following command:

```
export TERM=xterm
```

Adding the Database to the Application

We have this fancy new database created and linked to our application, but we aren't using it in our source code yet. In order to use the database we must first add a dependency for the database driver in our maven *pom.xml* file. Open up the file in your favorite IDE or editor and add the following section after the *</properties>* tag:

```
<dependencies>
        <dependency>
            <groupId>org.postgresql</groupId>
            <artifactId>postgresql</artifactId>
            <version>9.4-1200-jdbc41</version>
        </dependency>
</dependencies>
```

Once the dependency for the PostgreSQL driver has been added, we need to modify our *InsultGenerator.java* source file to connect to and run queries against the new database. Open this file in your IDE or text editor and replace the contents with the following:

```
package org.openshift;

import java.sql.Connection;
import java.sql.DriverManager;
import java.sql.ResultSet;
import java.sql.Statement;

public class InsultGenerator {
  public String generateInsult() {
    String vowels = "AEIOU";
    String article = "an";
    String theInsult = "";


    try {
```

```
String databaseURL = "jdbc:postgresql://";
databaseURL += System.getenv("POSTGRESQL_SERVICE_HOST");
databaseURL += "/" + System.getenv("POSTGRESQL_DATABASE");

String username = System.getenv("POSTGRESQL_USER");
String password = System.getenv("PGPASSWORD");
Connection connection = DriverManager.getConnection(databaseURL, username,
password);

if (connection != null) {
  String SQL = "select a.string AS first, b.string AS second, c.string AS noun
  from short_adjective a , long_adjective b, noun c ORDER BY random() limit 1";
  Statement stmt = connection.createStatement();
  ResultSet rs = stmt.executeQuery(SQL);
  while (rs.next()) {
   if (vowels.indexOf(rs.getString("first").charAt(0)) == -1) {
    article = "a";
   }
   theInsult =  String.format("Thou art %s %s %s %s!", article,
   rs.getString("first"), rs.getString("second"), rs.getString("noun"));
   }
   rs.close();
   connection.close();
 }
} catch (Exception e) {
 return "Database connection problem!";
}
 return theInsult;
 }
}
```

Don't worry if you don't want to type in all of the above source code. You can find this modified application on GitHub (*https://github.com/gshipley/book-insultapp-final*).

Once you have made the changes, committed them, and pushed them to your public GitHub repository, it's time to start a new build to deploy the new version of the source code. This can be done by clicking on the *Start Build* button while looking at the builds in the web console. Alternatively, you can start a new build using the *oc* tool with the following command:

```
oc start-build insults
```

Once the build has finished, verify that your application is working by viewing it in the web browser.

Adding a REST Endpoint

We are on a roll with adding additional functionality to our application so let's keep this train chugging down the tracks. The last thing we want to add to our insult generator is the ability to return an insult as a JSON document. Having an HTTP-based endpoint that provides the response in JSON will allow those that prefer to parse their insult with all the luxury they have come to expect when working with JSON documents.

The first thing we want to do is add a dependency for Java EE that allows us to use JaxRS to generate the results. Open the *pom.xml* that we modified previously in this chapter and add the following dependency:

```
<dependency>
    <groupId>javax</groupId>
    <artifactId>javaee-api</artifactId>
    <version>7.0</version>
    <scope>provided</scope>
</dependency>
```

Now that we have our dependency added to our *pom.xml* file, it's time to add two Java classes that will expose the endpoint. The first one is a simple *JaxrsConfig.java* file that specifies the application path our services will reside on. Create a new file called *JaxrsConfig.java* in the */src/main/java/org/openshift* directory and add the following code:

```
package org.openshift;

import javax.ws.rs.ApplicationPath;
import javax.ws.rs.core.Application;

@ApplicationPath("/api")
public class JaxrsConfig extends Application{
}
```

The last thing we need to do is define our endpoint that will return the insult. Create a new file named *InsultResource.java* under the */src/main/java/org/openshift* directory with the following source code:

```
package org.openshift;

import java.util.HashMap;
import javax.enterprise.context.RequestScoped;
import javax.ws.rs.GET;
import javax.ws.rs.Path;
import javax.ws.rs.Produces;

@RequestScoped
@Path("/insult")
public class InsultResource {

  @GET()
  @Produces("application/json")
  public HashMap<String,String> getInsult() {
  HashMap<String, String> theInsult = new HashMap<String, String>();
  theInsult.put("insult", new InsultGenerator().generateInsult());
  return theInsult;
```

```
    }
  }
```

These two source files will expose an endpoint at the /api/insult URL and listen for GET requests. Once a request is made, a JSON document will be returned with an insult that is provided by the PostgreSQL database we added earlier in this chapter.

Once you have code added, committed, and pushed to your repository, start a new build on OpenShift. Once the build has completed, browse to your endpoint and you should see the following JSON response:

```
{"insult":"Thou art a dankish weather-bitten minnow!"}
```

Summary

In this chapter, we learned how to add a database to an existing project. Once we added the database, we learned how to link the database to an existing deployment configuration inside of the project. We also learned how to use the terminal from the web console to import schema into the database. In the next chapter, we look at how to scale up your application to handle more users, and how to automate aspects of the deployment of your application.

CHAPTER 6

Deploying and Scaling Your Application

By now you have successfully deployed both the *Hello, World* and *Insults* applications based on the WildFly application server for Java. applications aren't static and as you continue to make changes you will want to keep redeploying the application. We already showed you how you can manually trigger a rebuild and redeployment of your application, but doing that all the time can get repetitive. In this chapter we discuss how to define triggers so that any time you push changes to your code repository on GitHub, your application will be automatically rebuilt and redeployed. We will also look at how to scale your application, deployment strategies when releasing new versions, application health checks, and rollbacks.

Automatic Deployments Using Webhooks

A webhook (also called a web callback or HTTP push API) is a way an application can provide other applications with real-time information or notifications.

We can configure the GitHub code hosting service to trigger a webhook each time we push a set of changes to your project code repository. Using this tool, we can notify OpenShift when you have made code changes and thus initiate rebuild and redeployment of our application.

Adding Our Webhook URI to GitHub

Before we can configure GitHub with a webhook for your application, we need to first find the webhook URI for your particular application:

1. Navigate back to the *Builds* page for the *helloworld* application in the OpenShift web console. But this time click the *Configuration* tab (see Figure 6-1).

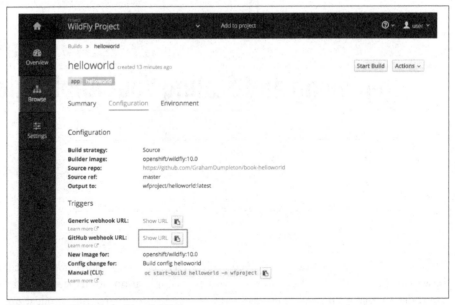

Figure 6-1. GitHub webhook URL

2. In the *Triggers* section you will find two different types of webhook URLs specified: *Generic webhook URL* and a *GitHub webhook URL*. Since we are going to configure GitHub with a webhook, select and use the *GitHub webhook URL*.

3. Head to GitHub and find the code repository created when you originally forked the *helloworld* project. Find the *Settings* tag and select it, as shown in Figure 6-2.

Figure 6-2. Settings on GitHub

4. Next, select the *Webhooks & services* option, as shown in Figure 6-3.

Figure 6-3. Webhooks & services on GitHub

5. Then the *Add webhook* button, as shown in Figure 6-4.

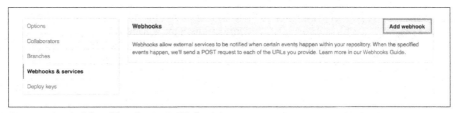

Figure 6-4. Add webhook on GitHub

6. This will bring you to the page where you can enter the callback URL for the webhook. At this point you should copy and paste the *GitHub webhook URL* from the *Builds* page of the OpenShift web console into the *Payload URL* field, as shown in Figure 6-5.

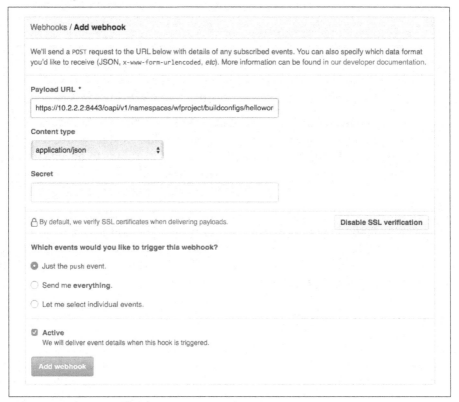

Figure 6-5. Setting callback URL on GitHub

7. Finally, you can select the *Add webhook* button.

If your OpenShift instance has been set up with a self-signed SSL certificate for HTTPS connections, you will need to select *Disable SSL verification*. If this is not done, GitHub will first attempt to verify the SSL certificate when connecting, which for a self-signed certificate will fail.

Visibility of Your OpenShift Instance

At this point, whenever you push a code change to your GitHub repository for your application, the application will be automatically rebuilt and deployed. But we do though have to admit to a slight fib.

For the webhook mechanism to work, your OpenShift instance must be visible from GitHub. In other words, the OpenShift instance must be hosted on a publicly visible URL.

In this book, we use the all-in-one VM image running on your own machine. Although we use the *xip.io* service to give the impression that your application is accessible over the public Internet, it isn't really and can only be accessed from your local system. This is because the IP address 10.2.2.2 is actually a private address.

Sorry for this slight detour, but we wanted to explain all the required steps. That way when you are using an OpenShift instance that is visible to your source code repository service, you will still know how to set it up. If you want to be able to use this feature using the all-in-one VM, you will need to use a webhook proxy service such as Ultrahook (*http://www.ultrahook.com*).

Finally, although we have provided an example here for setting up GitHub, other source code repository services are also supported. You will just need to work out whether they make use of a webhook mechanism compatible with GitHub, or if they can be set up to generate a callback suitable for use with the *generic webhook URL* endpoint. Use whichever is appropriate for your service.

Scaling Your Application

You are now in a position to make code changes to your application and have it automatically deployed. So far, we've been running with a single instance of your application. WildFly, upon which your application is based, can scale up to handle a high number of connections, but eventually you may hit a limit on the amount of CPU resources available to you if resource limits have been defined for a pod.

In order to handle the greater load you will need to scale out the number of instances of your application. But don't fear—OpenShift makes this an easy task. All you need to do is specify the number of replicas of your application that you want running.

OpenShift will then work out the best place to run your application, as well as set up routing to load balance requests across as many copies as you have.

Scaling from the Web Console

Scaling up the number of instances of your application running can be done from the *Overview* page for your application in the OpenShift web console (the page with those tell-tale up and down arrows we saw previously). Jump to that page and click the up arrow key twice to increase the replica count to 3, as shown in Figure 6-6.

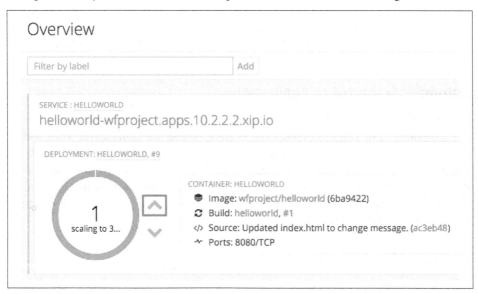

Figure 6-6. Scaling up

Once you do this, you will see the tracker for the number of instances running change as the target number is updated and the new instances are started. Once they are all running, you can reduce it again by selecting the down arrow.

Decreasing the number of replicas down to zero is possible, but OpenShift will display a popup to confirm the action. This is because reducing the replica count to zero is the same as putting your application offline. If users try to connect, the OpenShift router will still accept the connection, but will return a HTTP 503 Service Unavailable error because there will be no copy of your application to route traffic to.

If you were running a production application it would be better to put up a maintenance page indicating a planned outage, but if you needed to take a site down in a hurry over security concerns or some other reason, reducing the replica count to zero is an easy way to do it.

Applications Suitable for Scaling

Although OpenShift will let you scale up any application you may have started, you do need to ensure that any application is safe to scale up to more than one instance.

If your application is a web application that adheres to the 12-factor methodology (*http://12factor.net*), or what might also be called a cloud native application, then it would generally be safe to scale up.

Applications that can't usually be able to be scaled up include traditional relational databases backed by persistent storage. Databases cannot be scaled in the traditional way as only the primary instance of the database should have the ability to update data. Scaling can still be performed, but usually only on read-only instances of the database.

Automatic Scaling of an Application

In the previous section, we manually scaled up the application from the web console, but OpenShift also supports automatic scaling. While we don't cover auto scaling here, it works by defining upper and lower thresholds for CPU usage by pod. If the upper threshold is consistently exceeded by the running pods for your application, a new instance of your application will be started. When CPU usage drops back below the lower threshold, because your application is no longer working as hard, the number of instances will be scaled back again.

Deployment Strategies

A deployment strategy defines the process by which a new version of your application is started and the existing instances shut down. By default OpenShift uses a rolling deployment strategy that enables you to perform an update with no apparent down time.

But this default strategy isn't suitable for all applications, so it is important to understand all the strategies available so you can be sure you are using the correct one.

Rolling Strategy

A rolling deployment slowly replaces instances of the previous version of an application with instances of the new version of the application. A rolling deployment can wait for new pods to become ready via a readiness check before scaling down the old instances. Such a readiness check allows a rolling deployment to be aborted if a problem occurs.

This is the default deployment strategy in OpenShift. Because it runs old and new instances of your application in parallel and balances traffic across them as new instances are deployed and old instances shut down, it enables an update with no down time.

As you make code changes, when deploying the new version of your application you have to consider whether the new code will work with the existing data stored in a database. If old and new code require different versions of the database model, you should not use the rolling strategy.

Also remember what we said previously about scaling up applications. For some applications it wouldn't be safe to run more than one instance at any time, even if there had been no code changes.

A rolling deployment is therefore not suitable where multiple instances of the same application cannot be run at the same time, or where instances of both old and new code cannot be run at the same time.

Recreate Strategy

Rather than starting up new instances of your application while still running old instances, the recreate strategy first shuts down all running instances of the old application. Only after all the old instances of the application have been shut down will the instances using the new code be started.

This strategy should be used where you cannot run more than one instance of your application at the same time, or where you cannot run instances using old and new code at the same time. If you were running a traditional relational database, you would typically use this deployment strategy. It should also be used for a front-end web application when you need to perform a database migration as part of the deployment. We will talk more about database migrations later when discussing life-cycle hooks.

With this strategy, as all old instances of the application will be stopped before deploying instances with the new code, there may be a period of time when your application is not available. Unless you have taken steps to first route traffic to a temporary application that shows a maintenance page, users will see a HTTP 503 Service Unavailable error response.

Changing the Strategy

At the time of writing, to change the deployment strategy we need to drop below the covers of what the OpenShift web console and command-line tools provide direct support for and edit the *Deployment Configuration* directly. To do this we are going to use the oc edit command:

```
oc edit dc/insults -o json
```

This command will start up an editor displaying the deployment configuration in JSON format. Find in the deployment configuration the "strategy" subsection located under the spec section. Replace this definition, substituting `"Recreate"` for the `"type"` attribute, as shown here:

```
"spec": {
    "strategy": {
        "type": "Recreate"
    },
```

Implementing Custom Strategies

In addition to these two basic deployment strategies, various other more complicated strategies can be implemented including Blue-Green or A/B deployment strategies. These can be implemented by using multiple deployment configurations and reconfiguring what pods are associated with the exposed service for an application using labels. Custom strategies like this can be set up manually, or you can provide an image that embeds the logic for handling a deployment and that interacts with OpenShift via the REST API to make the changes in resources associated with the application.

Application Health Checks

Your application is starting up okay, but how can you monitor it to know whether it is actually ready to handle requests? Even if it starts out handling requests okay, how can you know whether it fails at some point and stops handling new requests? This is where high-level application health checks come in.

Two primary types of health checks are provided: a readiness probe and a liveness probe.

The readiness probe is used to determine if a new instance of your application is running properly before reconfiguring the router to send traffic to it, while a liveness probe is run periodically once traffic has been switched to an instance of your application to ensure it is still behaving correctly. If the liveness probe fails, OpenShift will automatically shut down that instance of your application and replace it with a new one.

Both types of probes can be implemented three different ways:

HTTP check
  The container is considered healthy if a HTTP request against a defined URL returns with a HTTP 200 or 399 status code.

Container execution check

The container is considered healthy if a defined command run inside of the container returns with a *0* exit status.

TCP socket check

The container is considered healthy if a connection can be established to the exposed port of the application.

You can check the deployment logs for details of any errors in the event that a probe fails.

Try adding an HTTP type readiness probe check to the *Insults* application using the command:

```
$ oc set probe dc/insults --readiness --get-url=http://:8080/healthz
deploymentconfig "insults" updated
```

Because a configuration change was made, a new deployment will be triggered immediately. On the *Overview* page, you will see the new deployment being run, displayed above the existing one and marked as *In Progress*, as shown in Figure 6-7.

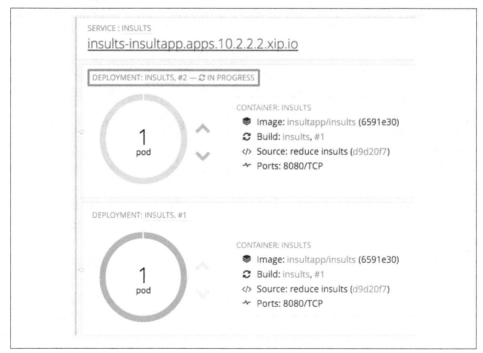

Figure 6-7. Readiness probe

The new deployment will stay in this state for a period, eventually moving to a failed state, because although we added a readiness probe, the application doesn't provide one at that URL. As a result the application always returns an HTTP status code of 404.

But change the HTTP URL for the readiness probe to be the root URL for the site:

```
$ oc set probe dc/insults --readiness --get-url=http://:8080/
deploymentconfig "insults" updated
```

and you will see the failed deployment removed and yet another new deployment performed. Because this time the readiness probe uses a valid URL that returns a 200 HTTP status code, it will be seen as ready, with traffic switched to the new instance and the old instances shut down.

Readiness probes can be used to check whether a new instance of your application is running okay before switching traffic to it, thereby reducing the chance that your new application is broken causing your site to be unavailable.

Deployment Lifecycle Hooks

Health checks are great for determining if your application is running okay. But what if you require special steps as part of your deployment? This is what lifecycle hooks are for.

An example of a step you might run would be to set a database flag to cause a site maintenance page to be put up by your web application at the start of the deployment, with it removed once the deployment is complete. You could also use an appropriate lifecycle hook to run a database migration, although keep in mind what we said earlier about the different types of deployment strategies and find the one most suitable for your project.

There are three different types of lifecycle hooks available:

Pre
> This hook is executed before any new instance of your application for a deployment is started and also before any old instances have been shutdown.

Mid
> When using the *Recreate* deployment strategy, this is executed after all old instances of your application have been shut down, but before any new instances of your application have been started. This hook is usually used where you can safely run any database migrations.

Post
> This is executed after all instances of your application for a deployment have been started and old instances have been shut down.

Both of the applications we have deployed so far use the *rolling* deployment strategy. Let's configure the *Insults* application with both a *pre* and *post* hook so you can see when a new deployment is starting and when it finishes.

As before when updating the deployment strategy, to set a deployment lifecycle hook we use the `oc edit` command.

Run this command again:

```
oc edit dc/insults -o json
```

From the editor find the "strategy" subsection under the deployment configuration `"spec"` section. We are going to restore this to a rolling deployment strategy. To that we are then going to add `"pre"` and `"post"` sections under `"rollingParams"` to yield:

```
"spec": {
    "strategy": {
        "type": "Rolling",
        "rollingParams": {
            "pre": {
                "failurePolicy": "Abort",
                "execNewPod": {
                    "command": [
                        "/usr/bin/echo",
                        "RUNNING PRE HOOK"
                    ],
                    "containerName": "insults"
                }
            },
            "post": {
                "failurePolicy": "Abort",
                "execNewPod": {
                    "command": [
                        "/usr/bin/echo",
                        "RUNNING POST HOOK"
                    ],
                    "containerName": "insults"
                }
            }
        }
    },
```

Adding lifecycle hooks will not automatically cause a redeployment, so trigger a new deployment by running the `oc deploy` command:

```
$ oc deploy insults --latest
Started deployment #10
```

This time when deployment occurs, a transient instance of the `insults` container for your application will be started and the command defined by the lifecycle hook run.

You can watch the progress as the containers are started and stopped using the `oc get pods` command:

```
$ oc get pods --watch
insults-10-deploy      0/1       Pending       0            3h
insults-10-deploy      0/1       Pending       0            3h
insults-10-deploy      0/1       ContainerCreating   0            3h
insults-10-hook-pre    0/1        Pending       0            3h
insults-10-hook-pre    0/1        Pending       0            3h
insults-10-hook-pre    0/1        ContainerCreating   0            3h
insults-10-deploy      1/1       Running       0            3h
insults-10-hook-pre    0/1        Completed     0            3h
insults-10-rbo58       0/1       Pending       0          3h
insults-10-rbo58       0/1       Pending       0          3h
insults-10-rbo58       0/1       ContainerCreating   0          3h
insults-10-rbo58       0/1       Running       0          3h
insults-10-rbo58       1/1       Running       0          3h
insults-9-sc3fz        1/1     Terminating   0            3h
insults-9-sc3fz        1/1     Terminating   0            3h
insults-10-hook-post   0/1        Pending       0            3h
insults-10-hook-post   0/1        Pending       0            3h
insults-10-hook-post   0/1        ContainerCreating   0            3h
insults-10-hook-post   0/1        Completed     0            3h
insults-10-deploy      0/1     Completed     0            3h
insults-10-deploy      0/1     Completed     0            3h
insults-10-hook-post   0/1        Completed     0            3h
insults-10-hook-pre    0/1        Completed     0            3h
insults-9-sc3fz        0/1     Terminating   0            3h
insults-9-sc3fz        0/1     Terminating   0            3h
```

The containers in which the lifecycle hooks are run are short-lived and are automatically cleaned up. But if you are quick enough you should be able to capture the messages logged from the corresponding pod using the `oc logs` command or from the OpenShift web console. We will talk about the `oc logs` command and how to use it in a later chapter.

Try experimenting with the *post* hook, replacing the command with */usr/bin/false*. This will cause the overall deployment to fail and everything will be automatically rolled back to the previous successful deployment.

Application Rollback

When using the readiness process with a lifecycle hook, if the check or action fails, deployment will not proceed and everything will be returned to the previous state.

If deployment was successful, but you later find the application is failing in some way due to the latest code changes, you will likely need a way to roll back to the last known good version of your application.

To get a list of all the deployments that have been made, you can use the following:

```
oc describe dc/insults
```

Look for the list of deployments and find the last deployment before the current one, which is marked as complete. You can roll back to this version using the `oc rollback` command:

```
$ oc rollback insults --to-version=10
#12 rolled back to insults-10
Warning: the following images triggers were disabled: insults:latest
  You can re-enable them with: oc deploy insults --enable-triggers -n insultapp
```

As noted in the command output, rolling back to a prior version will disable image change and configuration change triggers. After addressing any issues and running a new build, you will need to re-enable the triggers when starting the next deployment.

Summary

In this chapter, we introduced you to scaling and deployments. Many chapters could be written on these topics alone, but we wanted to keep things as simple as possible. You should have at least got a glimpse of the power that is available to you through these features, as well as the `oc` command-line tool. We will look more at the `oc` command-line tool and how it can be used to manage your application later on.

CHAPTER 7

Using Application Templates

One of the first things a developer does when starting a new job or when deciding to work on a project already in progress is to spend a good deal of time just getting their environment set up and configured. This can take hours, days, or even a week depending on the complexity of the project before they are able to run a full build and deploy of the application assets. But wouldn't it be nice if a new developer could get a working environment up in a matter of minutes? This was our goal with application templates on the OpenShift platform, and we have made some great progress. In this chapter will we explain what an application template is and how to use it.

What Is an Application Template?

The official OpenShift 3 documentation (*http://red.ht/1NVyUGr*) states:

> A template describes a set of objects that can be parameterized and processed to produce a list of objects for creation by OpenShift. The objects to create can include anything that users have permission to create within a project, for example services, build configurations, and deployment configurations. A template may also define a set of labels to apply to every object defined in the template.

This means that typically a template will include:

- A set of resources that is created as part of "creating/deploying" the template.
- A set of values for the parameters defined in the template.
- A matching label attached to each of the generated resources that provides a convenient way to indicate the resources are connected.

A template will be defined in JSON or YAML format, and will be loaded into OpenShift for user instantiation, also known as application creation.

Templates can have global visibility scope (visible for every OpenShift project) or project visibility scope (visible only for a specific project).

Benefits of Using Templates

A template provides developers with an easy way to create all the necessary OpenShift resources for their application to work with minimal effort. This allows you to quickly deploy an application without having to understand all the underlying technology of the OpenShift 3 platform.

Using Our First Application Template

Now that we understand what an application template is and how it can beneficial to a developer, let's try using one. The application template we will be using will create a full Java EE application and a MongoDB database that will perform geospatial queries to update a map via REST endpoints. Sounds pretty complicated, right? Let's get this application stack up and running with just a few commands!

The first thing we want to do is create a new project to hold our application. Issue the following command:

```
oc new-project parksapp --display-name="Baseball Parks Application Stack"
```

Once you have a new project, you can add the template to the project namespace with the following command:

```
oc create -f https://raw.githubusercontent.com/gshipley/openshift3mlbparks/
master/mlbparks-template.json
```

This will make the template available only for the namespace that it was loaded to, in this case the project. If you want a template to be available to any user on the system, add it to the *openshift* namespace as the cluster administrator.

You can verify that the template was added by browsing to your project in the web console. You should see it displayed an as available option to deploy as shown in Figure 7-1.

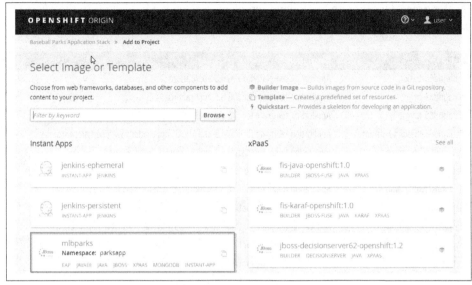

Figure 7-1. Templates

To deploy this application stack as running containers, simply click the template and then click the *Create* button. Your entire stack will be up and running in short order. Pretty awesome stuff, huh?

If you wanted to create an application based on the template you loaded from the command line, you would simply enter the following command:

```
oc new-app mlbparks --name="myparks"
```

There are many templates available today including ones for application stacks such as Wordpress as well as Node.js coupled with MongoDB.

We spoke briefly about namespaces as it relates to application templates. To show the available template for your current project, you can enter:

```
oc get templates
```

To show templates in another namespace you have permission to view, you can provide the *-n* switch. For example, the list of templates available to anyone on the system that have been loaded by the cluster administrator, issue the following command:

```
oc get templates -n openshift
```

At the time of writing, the following templates are loaded by default in the *all-in-one* image we are using:

Name	Description
datagrid65-basic	Application template for JDG 6.5 applications.
datagrid65-https	Application template for JDG 6.5 applications.
datagrid65-mysql	Application template for JDG 6.5 and MySQL applications.
datagrid65-mysql-persistent	Application template for JDG 6.5 and MySQL applications with persistent storage.
datagrid65-postgresql	Application template for JDG 6.5 and PostgreSQL applications.
datagrid65-postgresql-persistent	Application template for JDG 6.5 and PostgreSQL applications with persistent storage.
decisionserver62-amq-s2i	Application template for BRMS Realtime Decision Server 6 A-MQ applications.
decisionserver62-basic-s2i	Application template for BRMS Realtime Decision Server 6 applications.
decisionserver62-https-s2i	Application template for BRMS Realtime Decision Server 6 HTTPS applications.
eap64-amq-persistent-s2i	Application template for EAP 6 A-MQ applications with persistent storage.
eap64-amq-s2i	Application template for EAP 6 A-MQ applications built using S2I.
eap64-basic-s2i	Application template for EAP 6 applications built using S2I.
eap64-https-s2i	Application template for EAP 6 applications built using S2I.
eap64-mongodb-persistent-s2i	Application template for EAP 6 MongDB applications with persistent storage.
eap64-mongodb-s2i	Application template for EAP 6 MongDB applications built using S2I.
eap64-mysql-persistent-s2i	Application template for EAP 6 MySQL applications with persistent storage.
eap64-mysql-s2i	Application template for EAP 6 MySQL applications built using S2I.
eap64-postgresql-persistent-s2i	Application template for EAP 6 PostgreSQL applications with persistent storage.
eap64-postgresql-s2i	Application template for EAP 6 PostgreSQL applications built using S2I.
jenkins-ephemeral	Jenkins service, without persistent storage.
jenkins-persistent	Jenkins service, with persistent storage.
mongodb-ephemeral	MongoDB database service, without persistent storage.
mongodb-persistent	MongoDB database service, with persistent storage.
mysql-ephemeral	MySQL database service, without persistent storage.
mysql-persistent	MySQL database service, with persistent storage.
nodejs-example	An example Node.js application with no database.
nodejs-mongodb-example	An example Node.js application with a MongoDB database.
postgresql-ephemeral	PostgreSQL database service, without persistent storage.
postgresql-persistent	PostgreSQL database service, with persistent storage.

Creating Your Own Templates

As you have probably discovered by now, creating and using application templates is a very powerful tool to have at your disposal when developing software. The Open-Shift team has put in a tremendous amount of work to ensure that application templates exist and are usable today. The team is continually working on improving the creation flow so instead of trying to detail this here we refer you to the official Open-Shift documentation to ensure you are using the latest tools to create them. But if you just want to dive in head first, try the following command while inside of the project you want to create a template for:

```
oc export all --as-template=myapplication -o json > mytemplate.json
```

That should give you some JSON to get started with.

Summary

In this chapter, we learned about application templates and how to use them. We created a full Java EE stack with MongoDB using an application template. We then covered the available application templates provided out of the box with the *all-in-one* image. In the next chapter, we'll look at how you can determine what your application is doing when running and how to debug issues.

CHAPTER 8

Working with Your Application

Applications are great when they are working properly, but inevitably at some point most applications will need to be debugged. You might also need to tweak your application's build, or see what resources it has available. In this chapter we will dig into various tasks related to working with your application, whether as developer or as part of an operations team. While we have focused on using the OpenShift web console so far, in this chapter, we use the command-line tools so you can become more familiar with them.

Listing Running Instances

Information about running instances of your application can be found on the *Pods* page of the OpenShift web console.

If you want to find out what instances are running from the command line, you can use the `oc get pods` command:

```
$ oc get pods
NAME                  READY   STATUS      RESTARTS   AGE
helloworld-1-build    0/1     Completed   0          37m
helloworld-2-build    0/1     Completed   0          33m
helloworld-3-build    0/1     Completed   0          28m
helloworld-4-build    0/1     Completed   0          11m
helloworld-4-cd3y3    1/1     Running     0          9m
```

In this list, it is the pods with the *Running* status that are the instances of your application.

You can get a wealth of information about a specific instance using the `oc describe` command:

```
$ oc describe pod/helloworld-4-cd3y3
Name:        helloworld-4-cd3y3
```

```
Namespace:   wfproject
Image(s):    172.30.210.155:5000/wfproject/helloworld@sha256:9c941cb...
Node:        origin/10.0.2.15
Start Time:  Thu, 17 Mar 2016 11:30:08 +1100
Labels:      app=helloworld,deployment=helloworld-4,deploymentconfig=helloworld
Status:      Running
...
```

The labels are particularly important here. If you want to be more selective about
which pods are shown when running oc get pods, you can use the labels to narrow
your search:

```
$ oc get pods --selector app=helloworld
NAME                READY      STATUS     RESTARTS   AGE
helloworld-4-cd3y3  1/1        Running    0          21m
```

Running oc get pods by default shows you the current state of all the pods. If you
want to monitor the pods as they are created and destroyed in real time, use the --
watch option. This command will show all changes until the command is interrupted.

Container Logs

When an error occurs within your application, generally the first place you want to
look is in the log files. In OpenShift, there are two types of log files: the build logs and
the runtime application logs.

Build Logs

When OpenShift runs a build, it will capture the output of the steps run. This is the
case when using a S2I (Source-to-Image) builder as used for the WildFly application.
Build logs will also be available if you used OpenShift to build an arbitrary Docker
image from a Dockerfile.

The build logs can be accessed from the OpenShift web console by going to the *Builds*
page for your application. You can view the log live while a build is being run, or after
the build is complete.

If you want to access the build logs using the command-line tools, you first need to
identify which build you want to see the results for. You can see a list of all the builds
that have been completed using the oc get builds command:

```
$ oc get builds
NAME           TYPE      FROM          STATUS     STARTED           DURATION
helloworld-1   Source    Git@ac3eb48   Complete   23 minutes ago    2m8s
helloworld-2   Source    Git@ac3eb48   Complete   19 minutes ago    2m20s
helloworld-3   Source    Git@ac3eb48   Complete   15 minutes ago    2m15s
helloworld-4   Source    Git@master    Running    1 seconds ago     2s
```

To look at the logs for a specific build, you would then use the oc logs command. Prefix the name of the build with *build/* when identifying it:

```
$ oc logs build/helloworld-3
W0317 00:11:04.932223        1 builder.go:55] Master version ...
I0317 00:11:05.026730        1 source.go:197] Downloading "https://..." ...
I0317 00:11:10.187732        1 install.go:236] Using "assemble" ...
I0317 00:11:10.187908        1 install.go:236] Using "run" ...
I0317 00:11:10.187951        1 install.go:236] Using "save-artifacts" ...
Found pom.xml... attempting to build with 'mvn package -Popenshift ...'
Apache Maven 3.3.3 ...
Maven home: /usr/local/apache-maven-3.3.3
Java version: 1.8.0_71, vendor: Oracle Corporation
Java home: /usr/lib/jvm/java-1.8.0-openjdk-1.8.0.71-2.b15.el7_2.x86_64/jre
...
```

If a build shows as still running you can use the --follow option to the oc logs command to see updates to the log as they occur.

Application Logs

Application logs is what your application outputs when it is running. OpenShift will record any output from your application that is sent to the standard output and error streams.

The application logs can be accessed from the OpenShift web console by going to the *Pods* page and then to the pods for your application.

On the command line, to view the logs you should first list the pods for your application and then use the oc logs command for a specific pod:

```
$ oc logs helloworld-4-cd3y3
=========================================================================
  JBoss Bootstrap Environment
  JBOSS_HOME: /wildfly
  JAVA: java
  JAVA_OPTS: ...
```

This will give you the currently collected log output.

As with builds, if you want to monitor the log output live while that instance of your application is still running, you can use the --follow option to oc logs.

Application Startup Failures

If your application starts up and runs okay then you should always have some logs. But there is one special case you do need to be aware of—when your application fails to start up.

When your application fails to start up and exits, OpenShift will attempt to restart the application. If this keeps occurring, then the pod will be moved into a state called *CrashLoopBackOff.* You will see that a pod has entered this state when you use oc get pods to get a listing of the pods for your application:

```
helloworld-5-cqlo4        0/1        CrashLoopBackOff   2          1m
```

If you run oc logs on this pod, you will usually see a less than useful message.

```
$ oc logs helloworld-5-cqlo4
Error from server: Internal error occurred: Pod "helloworld-5-cqlo4" in
    namespace "wfproject": container "helloworld" is in waiting state.
```

This is a final error message from OpenShift resulting from the successive failures to start your application. This is not the log messages from your application.

In this case, to see the logs from the last attempt to start your application, you should use the --previous option with the oc logs command.

Environment Variables

In more traditional deployment environments, you would use a configuration file to customize the behavior of your application. When running an application under Docker, the problem is that you would need to rebuild the image for your application in order to make a change. This is because the configuration file is part of the Docker image.

To avoid needing to rebuild the image, you can use use environment variables set from outside the container. These could be environment variables that are directly understood by your application, or they could be environment variables that control additional command-line arguments supplied to the application server being used.

To see a list of what environment variables will be exported to a container when run by OpenShift you can use the oc set env command with the --list option to query the deployment configuration for your application.

```
$ oc set env dc/helloworld --list
# deploymentconfigs helloworld, container helloworld
PATH=/opt/app-root/src/bin:/opt/app-root/bin:/usr/local/sbin:/usr/local/bin:...
STI_SCRIPTS_URL=image:///usr/libexec/s2i
STI_SCRIPTS_PATH=/usr/libexec/s2i
HOME=/opt/app-root/src
BASH_ENV=/opt/app-root/etc/scl_enable
ENV=/opt/app-root/etc/scl_enable
PROMPT_COMMAND=. /opt/app-root/etc/scl_enable
WILDFLY_VERSION=10.0.0.Final
MAVEN_VERSION=3.3.3
```

To add or modify an environment variable, oc set env is once again used, but the environment variable name and value are supplied:

```
oc set env dc/helloworld MYSQL_DATABASE=mysql
```

If you want to update the value of more than one environment variable at the same time, each can be listed on the same command line separated by a space.

If you want to change more than one environment variable, then they should all be updated with the one command. This is because the configuration change will by default trigger a redeployment of your application with the new environment variables. Setting the environment variables one at a time would thus cause successive redeployments.

In addition to being able to update the environment variables when your application is run, if using the S2I builder, you can also specify the environment variables to be used when your application is being built. In this case, you need to update the environment variables on the build configuration for your application:

```
oc set env bc/helloworld MAVEN_ARGS_APPEND='-Dmaven.test.skip=true'
```

But be aware that when an environment variable is specified for a build configuration it will also be set when the container is run. This is because the environment variable is saved as part of the image. If an environment variable needs to have a different value at runtime than at build time, it needs to be set separately on the deployment configuration so that it overrides the value inherited from the build configuration.

Editing Configurations

Commands such as oc set env update the configuration for your application without you needing to know the details. Not everything you may need to do with a configuration can be done direct through the command line. Sometimes you may need to edit the configuration yourself.

In a previous chapter we used the oc edit command to add deployment lifecycle hooks. Using the oc edit command on a selected resource would start up an editor; the configuration is displayed within the editor and can be changed from the editor. You could then make changes and save the configuration, with it potentially triggering automatically a rebuild, a redeployment, or some other action.

Since configurations can be edited for many different reasons, we can't cover them all here. The OpenShift documentation goes into more detail, but there are a few specific resources that can be useful when editing configurations.

The first is the oc types command described back when we were introducing OpenShift. The text output of the oc types command is a quick cheat sheet for understanding the key concepts and types in OpenShift.

To understand what can be set in a configuration, take a look at the REST API documentation (*http://red.ht/1WKU0J6*).

A quicker way to get a description of what can be set is to use the oc explain command, which can be used on the name of a resource, or the path to a specific setting. The oc set env command, for example, updates the dc.spec.template.spec.containers.env setting. We can see a description for that by running the following:

```
$ oc explain dc.spec.template.spec.containers.env
RESOURCE: env <[]Object>

DESCRIPTION:
     List of environment variables to set in the container. Cannot be updated.

     EnvVar represents an environment variable present in a Container.

FIELDS:
   name <string> -required-
     Name of the environment variable. Must be a C_IDENTIFIER.

   value        <string>
     Variable references $(VAR_NAME) are expanded using the previous defined
     environment variables in the container and any service environment
     variables. If a variable cannot be resolved, the reference in the input
     string will be unchanged. The $(VAR_NAME) syntax can be escaped with a
     double $$, ie: $$(VAR_NAME). Escaped references will never be expanded,
     regardless of whether the variable exists or not. Defaults to "".

   valueFrom    <Object>
     Source for the environment variable's value. Cannot be used if value is not
     empty.
```

So we could have added or updated the environment variables by using oc edit instead of oc set env.

If using oc edit, by default the configuration will be provided as YAML. You can also edit it as JSON by supplying the -o json option to oc edit.

Debugging an Application

Even if your application starts up correctly you may find that it doesn't always behave as expected. This could be due to an issue with the runtime environment, or the configuration, whether that be a configuration file or environment variables.

In this case it can be useful to open up an interactive shell within the container where your application is running.

The command for running an interactive shell is oc rsh, but first you need to identify a running instance of your application. This is done using the oc get pods command, which we covered earlier. You can then use oc rsh on the selected pod:

```
$ oc rsh helloworld-8-fnzg5
sh-4.2$ env | grep OPENSHIFT
```

```
OPENSHIFT_BUILD_NAME=helloworld-6
OPENSHIFT_BUILD_SOURCE=https://github.com/GrahamDumpleton/book-helloworld.git
OPENSHIFT_BUILD_NAMESPACE=wfproject
OPENSHIFT_BUILD_REFERENCE=master
```

If you do not need an interactive shell and just want to run a command and have it return immediately, you can use oc exec:

```
$ oc exec helloworld-8-fnzg5 env | grep OPENSHIFT
OPENSHIFT_BUILD_SOURCE=https://github.com/GrahamDumpleton/book-helloworld.git
OPENSHIFT_BUILD_REFERENCE=master
OPENSHIFT_BUILD_NAME=helloworld-6
OPENSHIFT_BUILD_NAMESPACE=wfproject
```

The commands you have available to run within the container depend on what the Docker base image has provided. The ability to create an interactive shell when running oc rsh is dependent on a shell program existing as */bin/sh* within the image. Docker base images built with debugging in mind generally still provide you with common tools such as *ps, top,* and *vi.* A minimal Docker image may provide very few standard UNIX tools and you may find debugging more difficult, as oc rsh will not work if */bin/sh* is missing from the image.

Being able to bring up an interactive shell or run a command in the container your application is running is also obviously dependent on your application being able to run. We mentioned previously the case of where an application may not even start up. Some clues as to what is wrong in those cases can be using the oc logs command, ensuring the --previous option is used if the status of the pods has entered *Crash-LoopBackOff* mode.

To figure out why your application is having issues in this case you will not be able to use oc rsh or oc exec. Instead, use the oc debug command.

Whereas the oc rsh and oc exec commands are executed against a specific running instance of your application, the oc debug command is pointed at the name of the deployment configuration for your application. What the oc debug command will then do is start up an instance of the image for your application, but instead of running the normal application command, it will run an interactive shell instead.

```
$ oc debug dc/helloworld
Debugging with pod/debug-helloworld, original command: <image entrypoint>
Waiting for pod to start ...

Hit enter for command prompt

sh-4.2$
```

At this point your application has not been started. You can check that any required environment variables have been set, that any configuration files are correct, and that all your application files are present and correct. You can also start up your application and see why it is failing to start.

If you are using an S2I builder to build and deploy your application, this can usually be done by running the *run* script from the S2I scripts directory:

```
sh-4.2$ $STI_SCRIPTS_PATH/run
========================================================================
  JBoss Bootstrap Environment
  JBOSS_HOME: /wildfly
  JAVA: java
  JAVA_OPTS: ...
```

Deleting an Application

Finished working with the example applications in this book and want to remove all traces of them? There are a couple of ways this can be done.

If you only have the one application within the project namespace you are working in, the simplest way is to delete the whole project. This can be done using the oc delete project command.

```
$ oc delete project wfproject
project "wfproject" deleted
```

If you have other applications in the same project you want to keep, or wish to keep the project around after cleaning up the application, you need to be more selective about what is deleted. This is still a relatively easy task if the labels we mentioned earlier are used.

If you remember correctly, we used the *app* label of helloworld to list the pods corresponding to the instances of our application. We are going to use this same label to delete our application.

Before we do that, let's check to see what would be deleted by running the oc get all command with the selector and the *app* label.

```
oc get all --selector app=helloworld
```

This will output a list of everything that would be deleted if we used the same label. Once you know you aren't going to delete something you want, you can then run oc delete all with the same selector label:

```
$ oc delete all --selector app=helloworld
buildconfig "helloworld" deleted
imagestream "helloworld" deleted
deploymentconfig "helloworld" deleted
route "helloworld" deleted
service "helloworld" deleted
pod "helloworld-8-fnzg5" deleted
```

Summary

In this chapter, we took a quick look at some of the commands you can use to check on the state of your application, what is being logged, how to edit configurations as well as how to debug your application. This only scratches the surface of what you can do using the `oc` command-line tool. In the next chapter, we'll cover one further example, which is how to build and deploy an application using a Docker image. For further details on other tasks that can be performed using the `oc` command, run `oc help`. You can also use the `--help` option on specific commands for details about that command as well as examples.

CHAPTER 9

Deploying an Existing Docker Image

In the previous chapters we learned some key features of the OpenShift container application platform including the powerful source-to-image feature. If you recall, the S2I feature allows you to interact with the platform from a pure source code perspective. While this is awesome, there may be occasions when you want to deploy an existing Docker image to the platform. You will be happy to know that OpenShift supports this common request. After all, what good is a container platform if doesn't support the running of containers that have already been built? In this chapter we are going to deploy a Docker image from the public Docker Hub.

What Is Docker Hub?

If you are not familiar with Docker-based containers, chances are you haven't heard about Docker Hub before. Don't worry, it is a pretty simple concept to understand. However, to understand the need for Docker Hub, you first need to understand how a Docker image is actually built.

Unless they are using OpenShift, most developers don't have the luxury of a S2I project that automatically creates Docker images on the fly based on their source code. What this means is that when using plain Docker, a developer has to do a couple of things, namely create Dockerfiles and perform builds.

The Dockerfile

A Dockerfile is a text document that defines how an image should be created. Depending on the complexity of the application, the Dockerfile can quickly become verbose and unwieldy. As an example, here is the Dockerfile for the *official* popular Tomcat 8 servlet container:

```
FROM java:8-jre

ENV CATALINA_HOME /usr/local/tomcat
ENV PATH $CATALINA_HOME/bin:$PATH
RUN mkdir -p "$CATALINA_HOME"
WORKDIR $CATALINA_HOME

# see https://www.apache.org/dist/tomcat/tomcat-8/KEYS
RUN gpg --keyserver pool.sks-keyservers.net --recv-keys \
        05AB33110949707C93A279E3D3EFE6B686867BA6 \
        07E48665A34DCAFAE522E5E6266191C37C037D42 \
        47309207D818FFD8DCD3F83F1931D684307A10A5 \
        541FBE7D8F78B25E055DDEE13C370389288584E7 \
        61B832AC2F1C5A90F0F9B00A1C506407564C17A3 \
        79F7026C690BAA50B92CD8B66A3AD3F4F22C4FED \
        9BA44C2621385CB966EBA586F72C284D731FABEE \
        A27677289986DB50844682F8ACB77FC2E86E29AC \
        A9C5DF4D22E99998D9875A5110C01C5A2F6059E7 \
        DCFD35E0BF8CA7344752DE8B6FB21E8933C60243 \
        F3A04C595DB5B6A5F1ECA43E3B7BBB100D811BBE \
        F7DA48BB64BCB84ECBA7EE6935CD23C10D498E23

ENV TOMCAT_MAJOR 8
ENV TOMCAT_VERSION 8.0.32
ENV TOMCAT_TGZ_URL https://www.apache.org/dist/tomcat/tomcat-$TOMCAT_MAJOR/ \
v$TOMCAT_VERSION/bin/apache-tomcat-$TOMCAT_VERSION.tar.gz

RUN set -x \
        && curl -fSL "$TOMCAT_TGZ_URL" -o tomcat.tar.gz \
        && curl -fSL "$TOMCAT_TGZ_URL.asc" -o tomcat.tar.gz.asc \
        && gpg --verify tomcat.tar.gz.asc \
        && tar -xvf tomcat.tar.gz --strip-components=1 \
        && rm bin/*.bat \
        && rm tomcat.tar.gz*

EXPOSE 8080
CMD ["catalina.sh", "run"]
```

But wait, that doesn't look so complicated does it? Well, at first glance, this may appear to be true, but if you dig in just a bit further, you can see that this Dockerfile actually inherits the *java:8-jre* image. To really understand the image pipeline, you would also have to examine the *FROM* Dockerfile. The *FROM* Dockerfile contains the following information at the very top:

```
FROM buildpack-deps:jessie-curl
```

I have omitted the full Dockerfile for brevity's sake. If you would like to view the full Dockerfile for _java:8-jre, visit the official repository (*https://hub.docker.com/_/java/*).

What's interesting is that the *FROM* image for Java 8 is actually `buildpack-deps:jessie-curl`. The entire Docker image pipeline for a Tomcat server is as follows:

```
tomcat:8.0->_java:8-jre->_buildpack-deps:jessie-curl->debian:jessie
```

Working with Dockerfiles can certainly be helpful but it can also get confusing pretty quickly. Not only that, if you want to run the *official* Tomcat 8 Docker image, you have to dig in to the details just a bit to determine what underlying technology is actually being used. In this example, it appears that the Debian Linux distribution is used. While that may be fine for some, it may not be for others that are running in production.

Knowing you have a fully supported platform like OpenShift where you know the image pipeline is supported and verified by Red Hat can really ease any reluctance you may have about using Docker-based containers in a production environment.

The Docker Build

Once you have crafted that perfect chain of Dockerfiles, including one to actually copy their .war file into the container, a build is needed to actually create the image. The Docker build process is actually pretty simple once your Dockerfile is error-free. It can be performed with a command like the following:

```
$ docker build -t imagename .
```

This will resolve all of the *FROM* images in the Dockerfile chain and produce an image based on the Dockerfile in the current directory. Once the image has been created, you can tag the image to specify the version number.

Sharing the Docker Image

Whew, after all of that we now have a new Docker image. The next step is to actually share that image with other people so they can run it. This is where Docker Hub comes in.

In its simplest form, Docker Hub is a public repository where users can publish their images for use by others. Remember signing up for a GitHub account earlier in this book? Well, Docker Hub is like GitHub but for container images instead of source code.

Running a Docker Hub Image on OpenShift

You are probably going to send me mean and nasty email after you realize this entire chapter was written to introduce you to one single OpenShift command. That's okay, I probably deserve it, but I did think it was important for you to get a glimpse of the process of creating and distributing images. But at this point you probably just want to deploy the Tomcat 8 image, right? Good news. Open your favorite terminal and enter the following commands, assuming you have authenticated to your OpenShift server:

```
$ oc new-project tomcat8 --display-name='Tomcat 8'
$ oc new-app tomcat:8.0
```

You should see the following information after entering the preceding command:

```
--> Found Docker image b9c02aa (12 days old) from Docker Hub for "tomcat:8.0"
    * An image stream will be created as "tomcat:8.0" that will track this image
    * This image will be deployed in deployment config "tomcat"
    * [WARNING] Image "tomcat" runs as the 'root' user which may not be permitted
    by your cluster administrator
    * Port 8080/tcp will be load balanced by service "tomcat"
--> Creating resources with label app=tomcat ...
    ImageStream "tomcat" created
    DeploymentConfig "tomcat" created
    Service "tomcat" created
--> Success
    Run 'oc status' to view your app.
```

As you can see in the output, OpenShift realized that you wanted to use the Tomcat 8.0 image and it didn't have it in the OpenShift registry. Since the image wasn't available in the OpenShift registry, the platform then connected to the public Docker Hub registry to look for the image. Once it was found, it was downloaded (pulled) and stored in the OpenShift registry. Digging a bit deeper, the platform then extracted some meta-data and created Kubernetes objects for the image and finally deployed it inside of a pod.

Routes

Now that we have our fancy new public Tomcat 8 servlet container deployed to the platform, let's test it out. Open your favorite browser and log in to the OpenShift web console. Once you have been authenticated, you should see the projects shown in Figure 9-1.

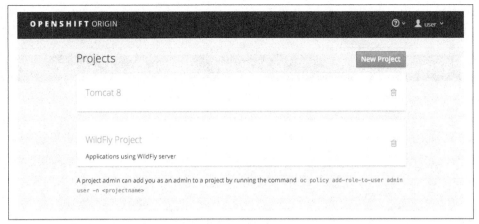

Figure 9-1. Projects

After clicking on the new *Tomcat 8* project we created on the command line, you will see the project overview page shown in Figure 9-2.

Figure 9-2. Project overview

What's different about this project compared to our first application using WildFly in Chapter 4? Give up? A route doesn't exist for the Tomcat 8 server yet. This means that although the Tomcat Docker image has been deployed in a container, it isn't yet accessible via the network. In order for Tomcat 8 to be visible, we need to expose the service as an external route. Routes are for externalizing the ports of an application or making it available as Internet facing. This is a fairly easy process. Simply click the

Create Route link inside of the *SERVICE* box. On the next page, you will be presented with the screen shown in Figure 9-3.

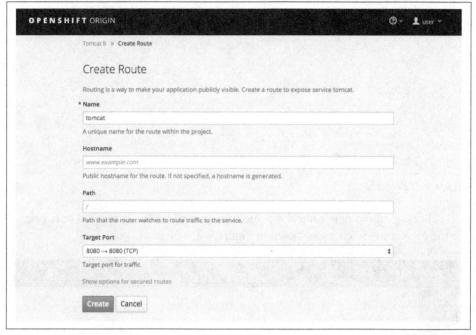

Figure 9-3. Create route

For this example, leave all of the values as they are and simply click the *Create* button. This will generate a default route using the *xip.io* service we discussed previously in this book.

After you click the *Create* button, you will now see that a route is displayed in the *SERVICE* box, as Figure 9-4 shows.

Figure 9-4. Exposed route

What are you waiting on? Go ahead, click the route. You will be greeted with the familiar Tomcat welcome page, as shown in Figure 9-5.

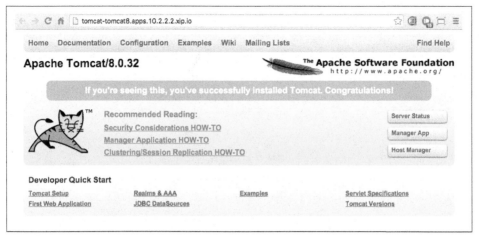

Figure 9-5. Tomcat application

Congratulations! You just deployed your very own Tomcat 8 server from the public Docker Hub. Want to scale this puppy up? Go ahead, knock yourself out.

While deploying this public Docker-based image was certainly cool, you have to consider what's missing here. The biggest thing to remember is that an image such as this doesn't take advantage of the platform's S2I build and deploy pipeline. This means you can't actually deploy code to the Tomcat container and have the build automatically happen. In this case, you would have to either create yet another Dockerfile that copies your built source code into the appropriate location or manually copy over a .war file into the running container. For that reason, you should use the S2I-enabled Tomcat 8 image that is shipped with the OpenShift platform. Using that builder image will save you a ton of time and headaches when deploying application code.

Summary

In this chapter, we learned a bit about the process to create and build Docker-based images. We also learned about Docker Hub and how to deploy an image that is hosted in a public external repository. Finally, we learned how to create a route so that the container can be accessed.

Afterword

All good things come to an end, and so we must now end this book. We hope you have enjoyed it and found it useful.

We know we could have filled many more chapters as we peeled back the layers of OpenShift, but our intent with this book was to get you up and running with the latest version of OpenShift as quickly as possible. We hope you will continue to explore the seemingly neverending possibilities of what a modern container application platform such as OpenShift can provide.

What We Covered

Here's what we covered:

- The components that go to make up a container application platform
- Basic terminology explaining the OpenShift components
- How to install your own copy of OpenShift
- How to create an application on OpenShift
- How to add persistent storage to your application
- How to automate the build and deployment of your application code
- How to scale up your application as you get more users
- How to choose the right deployement strategy for your application
- How to simplify application deployment using templates
- How to use application logs and debug deployment of your application
- How to use environment variables to customize your application's behavior
- How to deploy applications based on a Docker image

Final Words

The whole ecosystem that exists around container based deployment is still a rapidly evolving area. Standardization of key components is occuring under the umbrella of the Open Container Initiative (*https://www.opencontainers.org*) overseen by the Linux Foundation (*http://collabprojects.linuxfoundation.org*).

Even with the developing standards, there is still a large scope for products to distinguish themselves and offer unique functionality. To that end, the OpenShift team is commited to pushing the state of the art forward and provide you with a platform that we believe you will find compelling.

As we continue to develop OpenShift, check the OpenShift website and blog for the latest and greatest features. If you have suggestions for the platform you can always write to *openshift@redhat.com* or provide feedback via the OpenShift Origin (*https://github.com/openshift/origin*) project.

One of the things we love about working with OpenShift is that the more you use it, the more possibilities emerge—so the most important thing at this point is for you to get coding!

About the Authors

Grant Shipley is a Senior Manager at Red Hat focussed on cloud technologies. He has over 15 years of software development experience with Java and PHP. Grant also contributes to open source projects and builds mobile applications.

Graham Dumpleton is a Developer Advocate for OpenShift at Red Hat. He's an active member of the Python software developer community and the author of mod_wsgi, a popular module for hosting Python web applications in conjunction with the Apache HTTPD web server.

Colophon

The animal on the cover of *OpenShift for Developers* is a *black-headed caique* (*Pionites melanocephalus*), also known as the black-headed or black-capped parrot. They inhabit mostly humid forest areas in the Amazon (north of the Amazon River), Brazil (to the west of the Ucayali River), northern Bolivia, Colombia, Ecuador, French Guiana, Guyana, Peru, Suriname, and Venezuela.

The black-headed caique is medium-small with a short tail, black crown, yellow-orangeish head, white belly, yellow thighs, and green wings, back, and upper tail. Males and females have identical plumage; the only way to determine gender is through surgical sexing or DNA sexing—DNA sexing is much safer for the birds than the former. Wild caiques often have a brownish stained breast that is white on captive birds.

Black-headed caiques are often found in pairs or small flocks of up to 10 birds (sometimes up to 30). They mostly eat flowers, pulp, seeds, and possibly insects. The two subspecies of the black-headed caique—*P.m. melanocephalus* and *P.m. pallidus*—hybridize freely and often have similar coloring.

These birds are popular among parrot breeders and keepers. They make for energetic pets and require large cages filled with toys and perches. The minimum cage size recommended is 24" L × 24" W × 36" H with a maximum bar spacing of 1". Black-headed parrots use their beaks more than other parrot species and tend to bite. They mimic human speech poorly, often mimicking other sounds such as alarms, smoke detectors, microwave beeps, laughs, and whistles. Caiques also combine sounds in their vocabulary to form new sounds.

Many of the animals on O'Reilly covers are endangered; all of them are important to the world. To learn more about how you can help, go to *animals.oreilly.com*.

The cover image is from *Heck's Nature and Science*. The cover fonts are URW Typewriter and Guardian Sans. The text font is Adobe Minion Pro; the heading font is Adobe Myriad Condensed; and the code font is Dalton Maag's Ubuntu Mono.

CPSIA information can be obtained
at www.ICGtesting.com
Printed in the USA
FSOW04n1857150417
33051FS